Tips for Helping
Your Aging Parents…

WITHOUT LOSING YOUR MIND

KIRA REGINATO, CMC

ELDERCARE MANAGER, GERONTOLOGIST

Special discounts are available on quantity purchases.
For details, contact the author.
Kira@callkira.com
www.CallKira.com

Cover design by Lorna Johnson Print
Book design Lorna Johnson Print

Dedicated to my mom ~
a marvelous example of kindness
and integrity in this world

Contents

Introduction

You Can Do This!

Are you in a calm time, wondering how to prepare for the time when your parent starts needing assistance? Or, are you actively caring for an aging parent, handling one thing after another while fearing the next crisis?

Either way, this book is for you.

Helping parents can be rewarding, meaningful, and challenging. Being involved with our own lives, in addition to helping our parents, can send us around the bend, even though we love them.

I think eldercare today is an exhausting, emotionally taxing adventure, sprinkled with some life-changing loving moments and funny spells, too. This can be lonely work; often it's just one of us doing most of the assisting. Decades ago, we would have had many relatives close by to help. Add that to an inadequate and segmented medical and social service system and families are not getting the support they need and deserve.

 To watch a video I did called:
"Caregiving Ain't What it Used to Be" go to
https://youtu.be/uAqvE1kS3Ps

Sometimes I think of eldercare as a planet of its own and it's as though you've landed on this strange planet by accident. There is a strange language spoken, you don't know the currency or what things cost or how things work. And, many times you have to master this location during a crisis and learn quickly. Luckily, we have tour guides on Planet Eldercare called geriatric care managers.

Clients tell me they wish they had received professional help at the beginning because it would have led to better decisions. This book should help you minimize the common mistakes people make with their time, money, and energy when caring for a loved one as well as help guide you to professionals like a geriatric care manager who can solve many problems on Planet Eldercare.

This book is purposefully short, with easy-to-read sentences. I respect how busy you are and know that the role of caregiver is on top of everything else you are doing. I cared for my father for a couple of years so I'm sharing personal tips, as well as professional.

Ground Rules to Keep In Mind As You Read This Book

Help your parent in a gentle way, be patient with yourself and your siblings. This can be a long journey. No one gets it all right. Sometimes you have to allow good enough into the equation.

Keep in mind that you can't expect change from just one conversation. Keep the dialogue going.

Alternate the hard stuff and the easy stuff, so you don't overwhelm your parent or the others involved in caretaking. We don't want people to dread seeing you because you keep bringing up problems they don't want to face yet. Sometimes you have to let something drop until a window opens and allows renewed discussion.

Let yourself be helped. You don't have to go it alone.

In this book, I refer to Mom, Dad, and parent, but the advice applies to any older adult you may be helping. I know it's not grammatically correct, so I apologize here, but to avoid the s/he nomenclature, I refer to Mom, Dad, and parent as "they."

My secret plan is for you to be able to avoid crumbling under the role of caregiving. Caregiving can take a toll on your health and sanity and even on your finances. You probably know the health and mental effects, but the financial effects of taking time off work to care for a parent can be very costly. If using the tips in my book makes you healthier and wealthier when you age, that's cause for celebration!

With a hug of support,

Kira

Chapter 1

Your Future as a Caregiver

Since you're reading this book, chances are that you're currently a caregiver/care partner, even if you haven't called yourself that or thought of yourself in that role. You may have started to help but not thought about all you do or if you can continue. This chapter will help you quantify how you're helping and identify tasks that you prefer not to handle.

Maybe you have a good relationship with your parent but wonder how to set healthy boundaries and limits with your time.

Maybe you have conflicting feelings about helping your parents if they were neglectful, unhealthy, mentally ill, abusive, or just plain unhelpful when you were growing up. It may be difficult to give the time and attention to people who may not have done a very good job of caring for you.

Maybe you have resentment towards siblings who aren't helping enough.

Sibling Rivalry

This comes up frequently in the land of eldercare. Overbearing siblings and siblings with hidden agendas are common. If you can't handle this added stress, consider making an appointment for a consult with a geriatric care manager mentioned in Chapter 2. Having a professional working with the family to guide the design of a master plan minimizes family conflicts.

If siblings don't want to help or can't, maybe they can pay a person to do their part, or maybe you want to pay someone to do your part. That's an option if you have the funds.

Watch a movie about sibling rivalry in the RESOURCES section of this book.

From what I have observed, adult children are loyal and try to help, no matter their childhood experiences. Most of the time it's the parent who stonewalls.

To help you think more about the caregiver you are and want to be, complete the **Support System Questionnaire** at the end of this chapter. You may consider asking siblings to complete the **Support System Questionnaire** also.

Ideally you can all have a conversation about the answers and divide and assign responsibilities and tasks.

Before completing the **Support System Questionnaire**, keep in mind that there are costs to your health, time, and wallet when you're a caregiver.

Pitching in to help a parent can end up costing close to $300,000 for us over a lifetime due to lost wages and diminished contributions to pensions and Social Security (MetLife Study of Caregiving Costs to Working Caregivers).

An AARP study, "Family Caregiving and Out-of-Pocket Costs: 2016 Report," estimates that family caregivers spent an average of nearly $7,000 a year of their own money — **more than $7,400 in 2019 dollars.**

That spiked to nearly $12,000 - $12,700 when adjusted for inflation — for caregivers who lived an hour or more from the care recipient. Costs generally were slightly higher if those receiving the care were 50 or older.

Out-of-pocket spending is even higher among Hispanic/Latino caregivers ($9,022 annually, representing 44 percent of their income). African American caregivers report costs similar to white caregivers, but that amounts to a much greater percentage of income — 34 percent vs. 14 percent.

DAD NOTES: I would drive 80 miles round trip to take Dad to the VA for appointments in San Francisco. He always insisted we get there way early so we could grab breakfast. By the time we got there early for breakfast, had the appointment, did his labs, got him lunch, and came home, it might be six to eight hours altogether. Sometimes he would give me twenty dollars for gas and bridge toll and treat me to lunch. I lost hours of wages, but I wanted to be there for him, and he needed me to be there.

NOTE: The forms can be completed in this book.

In addition, if you prefer to complete them on a larger sheet of paper, you can order the set of forms that accompany this book in 8 1/2 x 11 format from **CallKira.com** for $4.95. This format will make them easier to complete and to include copies in your binders.

SUPPORT SYSTEM QUESTIONNAIRE

What are you good at? What do you want to do on behalf of your loved one? (For example: phone work, attending medical appointments, shopping, bill paying, researching insurance, cooking, etc.) _____

_____

_____

_____

_____

How many hours per week would you estimate you spend on caregiving responsibilities? (For example: driving, running errands, preparing meals, handling medication, doing hands-on care, etc.) _____

_____

_____

_____

_____

Are you able and interested in continuing that amount of time on caregiving responsibilities? _____

_____

_____

_____

_____

If not, what amount of time would be realistic? _____

_____

_____

_____

_____

What help do you think your loved one could use that s/he isn't receiving? _____

_____

_____

_____

_____

What would you prefer to have others do, even if that person has to be paid? _____

_____

_____

_____

_____

If only my loved one knew: _____

_____

_____

_____

_____

_____

_____

_____

Name: _____

Relationship: _____

Date: _____

Your parent can fill out a different questionnaire (on the following page) which can help articulate thoughts they may not easily share otherwise.

Discussing the answers to what you and your parent write allows you to learn each other's expectations. Even if you don't discuss each other's answers, the pot will have been stirred with food for thought.

PARENT QUESTIONNAIRE

How many hours per week would you estimate your child/children spends on responsibilities on your behalf? (For example: driving, running errands, preparing meals, handling medication, doing hands-on care, calling insurance company, etc.) _____

_____

_____

_____

_____

Do you believe you need less, more, or different help than you're getting? _____

_____

_____

_____

_____

What type of assistance would you find helpful? _____

_____

_____

_____

_____

If you could change one thing about your current situation, what would it be? _____

_____

_____

_____

_____

Are you aware of any health issues that have surfaced for your child/ children since they began assisting you? _____

_____

_____

_____

_____

What are your plans/goals for the next year?_____

_____

_____

_____

_____

If only my loved one knew: _____

_____

_____

_____

_____

_____

_____

_____

_____

_____

Name: _____

Date:_____

Chapter 2

Using a Care Manager

My profession's title has changed over the decades. The current title is Aging Life Care Professional but you'll also see people practicing as geriatric care managers, eldercare managers and care managers. According to the national association, AgingLifeCare.org "An Aging Life Care Professional, also known as a geriatric care manager, is a health and human services specialist who acts as a guide and advocate for families who are caring for older relatives or disabled adults."

Since managing eldercare matters can be difficult, and we often choose to delay doing difficult things, you may be tempted to read this book and not take action. But not taking care of business can lead to crisis management, which may compound into worse outcomes requiring even *more* of your time to handle.

That's why I recommend having at least one meeting with a care manager. Most families call us in crisis but others call for a brief consult when they are trying to decide how to proceed and help a loved one. Others call us when they find themselves stuck or overwhelmed while in the midst of caring. You may appreciate a professional to turn to in this painful, complicated, emotional time.

Having a care manager means that you have a partner on your journey. You don't have to figure out what to do on your own or to reinvent the wheel. Talking about the issues with a professional can be helpful and save hours of effort down the line.

Reasons You Might Need a Care Manager

- You do not have the time to commit to parent care.

- You have a difficult relationship with your parent. Caring for a parent is extremely hard even if you have a great relationship. It can be intolerable if you have a poor one. In some cases, however, poor relationships actually improve through the caregiving experience. There is much to consider.

- You're an only child, and it's too much on your shoulders alone. The good news is that you get to make all the decisions without arguing with siblings. The bad news is that you get to make all the decisions. Plus, you "get" to be the only one going to appointments, managing finances, and going to the hospital to be medical advocate, fact checker, and comfort monitor, as well as head cheerleader, etc.

- You live long distance and your parent needs local support.

- You feel powerless. Maybe because it's hard to communicate or collaborate with your parent on their care.

- Your parent has a mental illness or personality disorder, even if not yet diagnosed. Add that to a broken hip or dementia symptoms, and it's a recipe for high stress, chaos, and fear or helplessness for everyone involved.

- Your family wants objectivity. Guidance is welcome from an expert about how things are likely to unfold in the months or years ahead as well as how to address the issues at hand.

- It's difficult dividing caregiving tasks among siblings or other family members.

NOTE: I often see a son-in-law or daughter-in-law get along with the parent better than the adult child. This makes sense because they don't have the history to deal with. A client said her nephew is the "Grandma Whisperer." He can handle Grandma just the right way. Use this to your advantage. I know how frustrating it is to see Dad agree to something your spouse suggests when he refused the same thing with you. But who cares? Let family members help; it's actually very wise and strategic.

Care Manager Services

- We conduct a professional assessment of the needs and strengths of your loved one and your family. We take into account the goals of the older adult.

- We listen to concerns and suggestions from spouses and adult children. We need to listen before we start solving problems. Decision-making is helped by separating the factual from the emotional.

- We provide immediate solutions so you can get relief.

- We guide families to the most appropriate and affordable options available.

- We create a care plan with suggested action steps and resources.

- We arrange for chosen services, saving you hours of time.

- We contact and consult with doctors and other health professionals, as needed.

- We arrange and monitor home care.

- We handle a discharge from the hospital or rehab facility.

- We accompany your parent to appointments as the advocate and note taker, and then provide follow-up.

- We coordinate moves from home to a care facility.

- We encourage completion of legal documents such as a trust, advance health care directive, will, etc.

- We arrange individual, couple, or family therapy. Some care managers are licensed to provide this in addition to care management services.

- We schedule appointments and transportation.

Care Managers Do NOT

- Diagnose physical or mental illness

- Prescribe or administer medications

- Direct medical or nursing care

- Provide physical, occupational or speech therapy

Anyone can hire a care manager: an adult child, the parent, a spouse, a grandchild. We can help long-term or provide a one-time consultation.

I was asked, "Can I hire you even if my mom and brother don't want your help? Every time I talk to you, I feel calm and I get direction." I said, "Certainly. We can always help individual members of the family, providing guidance and support."

Hiring a Care Manager

Call two or three care managers to compare, if you have choices in your area. Pick the one you can envision meeting your parent and working well with your family.

Ask each care manager:

- **How long have you been doing care management? Do you specialize?**
  You are looking for a professional who has a lot of experience dealing with your parent's set of issues such as dementia, disability, behavioral health, chronic illness, etc. The more experience, the better.

- **What are your credentials, degrees, or certification?**
  Consider a professional with education in gerontology (study of aging), social work, or nursing.

  NOTE: A professional care manager can choose to attain certain certifications. Often you will see CCM which stands for Certified Case Manager or CMC which is Care Manager Certified. However, no nationally standardized license or certification for geriatric care managers is required at this time.

- **Can you tell me about your response times?**
  I've found families working on eldercare concerns want a pretty immediate response from me in order to keep moving forward. You want to know emails and calls will be returned in a timely manner.

- **Fees?**
  Insurance and Medicare don't yet cover the costs for a care manager, unfortunately. Prices vary depending on where your parent lives. In my area of Northern California, care managers charge $100 to $200+ per hour, plus travel, and mileage in many cases.

- **Can you provide references?**
  Be sure to read the care manager's website and look for testimonials there.

  Call a reference.

Care managers try to be neutral and not to judge the way your family operates. We understand that family dynamics are entrenched and complicated, and that issues can't be solved overnight. We use discretion and acumen to gently push forward or advise letting issues go when discussions won't produce results.

Care managers have a complex job, but we enjoy being creative problem solvers.

Here's an email from a family member:

"Thank you! You really are so professional and have a nice light, positive air of clarity. You are just what I was hoping for to help us move through this scary time of caregiving options. I had been meeting a lot of resistance to moving forward, but know I feel I can relax and know we are going to move forward."

Visit AgingLifeCare.org to find a care manager in your area.

For more information on what a care manager does, see the article I wrote for *Tech Enhanced Life* under RESOURCES or watch the videos I did at the Commonwealth Club to explain my profession. https://youtu.be/GQ_NoZgFh0I.

The videos give you a real flavor of me because I use a lot of humor and case examples. My dad was in the audience that evening and so proud.

 To watch a video I did explaining what a care manager does, go to
https://youtu.be/GQ_NoZgFh0I

Chapter 3

Keep a Record

You may not know this, or want to hear this, but the average caregiver journey lasts four years. Yes, that can be a long time and some journeys last 10 to 20+ years. That's why I suggest people get a system in place as close to the start of the journey as possible.

Eldercare requires keeping track of loads of information. One way to get organized is to enter data into your smart device from the beginning OR begin a file on your computer and document all that transpires.

When you keep a running history of events, you don't need to try to keep it all in your head. If you're caring for more than one person, such as mom and dad, you may wish to keep a separate computer file for each.

What to Keep Track of Over Time

The main idea is that you want to capture health and life issues you may need to monitor. This does not mean you become a nag about things, because then your parent will become resentful. You just want to have awareness and be prepared and informed so you can be an advocate through the years.

Having notes to review allows you to look back and see patterns — falls, times in the hospital, upset stomach, pneumonia, etc. You can see the timeline of events and even let the doctor know when symptoms began.

It's good to take notes on conversations about events coming up and needs your parent has. Think about a timeframe to address them. Perhaps assistance is needed to handle things such as a driver's license renewal, getting a trust document made or revised, arranging for cataract-surgery transportation, that sort of thing.

Here are sample entries from my file when I was caring for my father:

DAD NOTES: 11/9 Dad went to VA. Blood work (fasting) showed elevated PSA, almost double, 2-4 now. VA to call him to go to SF appt. for more work. Needs records from 2004 surgery.

Eustachian tube blocked, needs to see ENT specialist in SF.

Got flu and tetanus shots.

12/16 Took Dad to beach. When I go to get him in apartment, he is wheezing, hard for him to dress, undies on inside out, suspenders backward. He refuses to let me turn them around, says they are on right.

Chapter 4

Medication Management

A key area of caregiving is knowing the medications your parent takes and checking to see they are taken as prescribed.

According to the Centers for Disease Control, "As people age, they typically take more medicines. Older adults (sixty-five years or older) are twice as likely as others to come to emergency rooms for adverse drug events (over 177,000 emergency visits each year), and nearly seven times more likely to be hospitalized after an emergency visit."

I noticed that the more ill my dad became, and the more meds he was prescribed, the harder it was for him to understand what he was taking or why. This is common.

DAD NOTES: My dad only took one medication for years: Lisinopril. When I asked him why he took it, he had no idea. When I asked, "Could it be for high blood pressure?" he would say, "Oh, no, I don't have high blood pressure." When I checked with his doctor, he verified that Dad had high blood pressure.

1. **Document Medications**
   Ask your parent if you can sit down and make a list of all current medications, vitamins, and supplements together. Search in each room and cabinet for meds because people rarely keep them all in one place. Medications might be in a kitchen drawer, a bedside table, or the bathroom.

If you find expired or unused meds, see if your parent will agree to get rid of them. Expired meds are toxic waste, so you can't just throw them in the garbage. The dump, pharmacy, police station, or hospital may accept them. If your parent refuses to dump old meds, put them in a remote place where they won't be taken by mistake.

BONUS: A discussion about medications gently opens the door to talk about your loved one's health problems.

Enter the completed medication list in your computer file and print a copy for the Hospital and Reference Binders you'll assemble in later chapters.

If you are using paper/pencil, use the form provided here.

Pharmacy Name: _____

Pharmacy Address: _____

Pharmacy Phone: _____

Pharmacy Fax: _____

ALLERGIES TO MEDICATIONS AND SUPPLEMENTS	
NAME OF MEDICATION	REACTION

MEDICATION LIST FOR:			
DATE:			
MEDICATION /SUPPLEMENT	DOSE	WHEN TAKING	WHY TAKING
Example: Lisinopril	*10 mg*	*AM*	*high blood pressure*

2. Organize Medications

Pill boxes can be purchased at pharmacies or online. Models vary depending on how many times meds are taken per day.

Take a team approach and fill the compartments with the medication for each day while your parent watches, or they can fill the container and you can watch. Two sets of eyes help prevent errors, such as missing or doubling up on a dose.

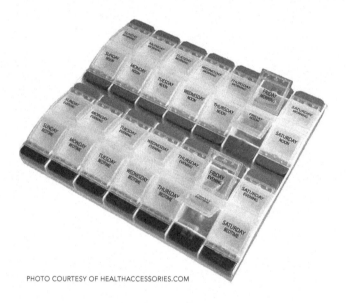

PHOTO COURTESY OF HEALTHACCESSORIES.COM

Develop a routine of filling the medication container weekly. Or, fill more than one container at a time and put the spare aside, ready to go.

Even if it's one pill a day, put it into the pill box. Include vitamins and over-the-counter meds. The earlier you and your parent get in the habit of using this system, the better the chance of reducing errors that can lead to hospital stays.

Keep all the medication bottles in one place. This way, when it comes time to fill the pill box, you have everything you need and can see when meds need to be reordered.

DAD NOTES: Initially, my dad refused to use a pill box, saying he could remember what to take when. After one hospital stay, however, when it was evident he was not taking meds as prescribed, I insisted. Once he used the box, he loved it and told me he had no idea how he could have managed without it. He told me repeatedly how happy he was to have my help managing his meds.

If medications and supplements are consistent, ask your pharmacist about a customized packaging system, such as pill packs or blister packs.

Pill packs organize medications by time of day and date. All pills (even vitamins) are packed in individually labeled disposable strips. Just simply tear off the pouch for that time of day.

With pill packs, there are no bottles to handle, no pill box is needed, and they are delivered to the home. PillPack.com is one of the companies offering this. You can ask your insurance company if they work with PillPack.com or a similar company.

There are also automatic, high-tech solutions for medication manage-ment such as robot dispensing machines sold by MedaCube, Hero, Livi, TabSafe, and MedReady (by Connect America), among others. The benefit of this type of machine is that about a month's worth of meds is placed into the machine and each dose is automatically dispensed at the correct time. A light and sound tell the person it's time to take their meds and a text or email can be sent to you if medications are not removed from the machine (and presumably taken). These machines can be especially helpful if your loved one has memory loss.

Chapter 5

Gather Documents

Now it's time to make a Reference Binder which can seem like a big task BUT your efforts will pay off when you realize how much you refer to these documents over time.

*Tell at least one other trusted person
where he or she can find this Reference Binder.*

If you're making the Reference Binder manually, here's what you will need:

- **Two 3-ring binders**
  (one binder will be used for making a Hospital Binder in Chapter 13)

- **Binder paper**

- **10 to 15 binder dividers**

- **Three-hole punch**

- **Package of five plastic sheets that hold standard 8 1/2" × 11" pages**

- **Plastic sheets designed to hold business cards**
  called Business Card Pages – available online or at office supply stores, as shown on following page

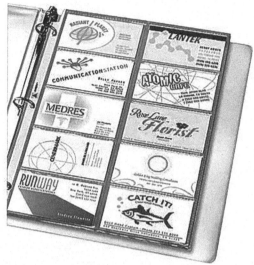

PHOTO COURTESY OF AVERY PRODUCTS CORPORATION

Assembling Your Reference Binder

1. **At the start of the binder, insert a business card page**
   Insert all business cards you have from professionals working with your loved one.

2. **Label a divider DOCTORS**
   If there are multiple doctors, you may want to label a divider for each doctor, noting the doctor's name or area of practice. Example: Dr. Tsu, Dr. Roman, etc., or Primary Doctor, Cardiologist. Place any documents you have from their offices into the binder for reference.

3. **Label a divider MEDICAL**
   Insert copies of lab results, medication instructions, discharge summaries from hospital stays, etc.

4. **Label a divider LEGAL**
   Ask about the location of important documents NOW. It can be challenging to find the document when an asset needs to be sold, as people forget the location.

Original documents may be stored in a safe deposit box or fireproof safe, etc. and it's also a good idea to keep a copy/picture of them so you can easily view the data when needed. Ensure that the location and the way to retrieve the documents is known by more than one person.

- Deed to property

- Birth certificate

- Marriage certificate

- Divorce certificate

- Title to car

- Driver's license

- Passport

- Trust

- Advance directive

- Power of attorney for finances

- Long-term care policy

- Life insurance policy

- Home insurance policy

It's good to keep a copy of the home insurance and life insurance policies as well as the car registration, so you can be sure they are paid up annually.

5. **Label a divider LONG-TERM CARE INSURANCE**
Place a copy of the policy here. You may need to refer to this over the years to read the fine print.

Read through the LONG-TERM CARE POLICY. It may cover in-home care, assisted living care, care in a nursing facility, OR a combination of these.

You may hear the term **ADLs** when working with medical and eldercare professionals. It stands for **Activities of Daily Living.**

The policy most likely will come into use when your loved one needs help with at least two Activities of Daily Living and/or has a dementia diagnosis.

There are six Activities of Daily Living:

• Bathing

• Dressing

• Going to the toilet

• Transferring (for example, getting up from a chair, out of bed, or out of a car to a wheelchair)

• Continence

• Feeding

Many policies have an elimination period, meaning a certain time-frame has to go by – often 90 days – before the company will begin to pay for coverage. If there is an elimination period, you want to be sure to get your loved one evaluated by the insurance company at the earliest time so that the clock can begin ticking on that unpaid period, thus allowing coverage as soon as the elimination period ends.

Consider calling the agent who sold the policy to have questions answered in advance of needing to use it and to identify when your loved one may qualify. The agent can be your ally when working with the insurance company and help you navigate that system at no charge.

· · · · ·

You may hear the term **IADLs** when working with medical and elder-care professionals.

This stands for **Instrumental Activities of Daily Living.**

There are typically eight Instrumental Activities of Daily Living:

- Meal preparation

- Using the telephone

- Shopping

- Driving

- Housework

- Financial management

- Medication management

- Driving

Either family helps or someone is hired to assist with these tasks. Unfortunately, insurance doesn't come into play when your loved one cannot perform some or all IADLs.

Chapter 6

Advance Health Care Directive

Purpose

All of us over 18 years old need to complete an Advance Health Care Directive (AHCD) in case we get to a point where we can't speak for ourselves or prefer someone else speak for us. It's not about finances; this one is just for medical decisions.

It's not about giving up control, either. IF you can make every medical decision for yourself until you die, you will. But if you ever need someone at your hospital bedside to make decisions, completing the form and naming an agent now will enable that to happen. An AHCD can serve *one or both* of these functions:

- Appoint an agent to speak for you (Power of Attorney for Health Care)

- Provide written instructions about your specific health care wishes

Where to Get a Form

Hospitals may have these forms as well as online organizations, such as NHPCO.org, Compassionandchoices.org, FiveWishes.org, and CoalitionCCC.org.

Completing a Form

Rest assured that forms come with instructions on how to complete them. Many hospice and palliative care organizations offer a workshop on completing the form.

The best approach I've found for completing the form is to sit down with your parent and fill it out *with* them. This opens up rich conversation about values and fears, as you discuss some difficult scenarios. You may be surprised at what your parent wants and doesn't want, too.

If possible, the health care agent your parent chooses should be local, objective, know your parent's health care wishes well, be calm in a crisis, and comfortable speaking with authority figures providing medical care.

Once the form is completed, you may want to make a short video on your phone with your parent recapping the important points. This way you have an accurate reminder of what your parent wants. You can watch it later if there are doubts or questions about what was said, or you just need to see your parent speaking their wishes, so you are fortified in acting on their behalf.

What to Do with Completed Form

- Once the form is completed, give a copy to your parent's doctor, for the chart.

- Provide a copy to the medical records department at their hospital of choice.

- Put a copy in the Reference Binder you made and the Hospital Binder you will be making.

It's good to remember that your parent has the right to change their mind about medical treatment or the person they named as their health care agent at any time. They just create a new AHCD and replace the old version with the new so the new one is on file with the correct sources.

CAUTION: If you wait too long, your parent may lose the capacity to legally complete or sign the document due to mental changes such as dementia. You want to complete a form and have conversations well in advance and as health changes come up.

Be Persistent

It took me two years to get my father to sign his AHCD. Many people are superstitious about discussing what could go wrong toward the end of life—thinking and talking about this stuff seems prohibited. Maybe Dad resisted for this reason, but who knows?

DAD NOTES: I would remind my dad to complete the form and he'd say, "Okay, just leave it there on the table." Then, nothing. I pleaded with him to fill out the darn form and he'd say, "You know my wishes." I did.

However, I also told him "Medical staff may not listen to me without a document proving to them that I'm your legal agent and therefore allowed to speak on your behalf." Still, he didn't complete the form.

So, one day, I just filled out the form, guessing at what he would have wanted. Then I handed the document to him when he was lounging outside, waiting for me to bring him lunch, and said, "Dad, sign this. If you don't, I won't bring you your sandwich!" He laughed and signed it, and I put it in the binder I kept for him, and that was that.

Chapter 7

Social Life

If you're concerned that your loved one is not engaging with others or activities lately, then check out the ideas below to address.

NOTE: Disengaging from social activities and/or an inability to manage one's social life is NOT typical. Seek medical advice if you suspect your loved one may be depressed or have early memory loss.

When next you see your loved one, start out by saying: I've noticed that lately you have been ... less active, not going out as much, bored, or ... See if that starts a conversation that can help guide how to solve the issue.

Since maintaining connection, feeling needed, and being with others is critical, suggest brainstorming together to identify ways to increase their social life.

Make a list of suggested activities together. Below are some to consider:

★ Offer to install **games** on computer such as chess with virtual partner or crossword puzzles, Sudoku, etc. Adjust font size, if needed, to make screen easier to see.

★ **Classes** such as learning a language, instrument, meditation, singing, cooking, yoga, walking tours, cards, pool, art, knitting, poker, armchair travel, dance lessons, or stuffing envelopes for a social cause.

★ We know that the number one thing a person can do to reduce the risk of dementia is to **exercise**. Getting the heart rate up puts extra oxygen and blood into the brain vessels, keeping them more healthy. With that in mind, check out exercise classes! Include fresh air and walking whenever possible, even if that means pushing a wheelchair outside.

Once you have some areas of interest for your loved one, see what is offered at community and senior centers as well as local colleges. Print out the options and review specifics with your loved one. They are more likely to say "yes" if you have a specific class, you do the leg work and registration and then invite them.

As much as you can, attend classes and activities for the first time or two so your loved one is not alone. Attending group activities promotes connection, new friendships, and combats loneliness. Oftentimes I'll drive and go with a client to bingo or an exercise class and then keep a low profile so they begin to talk with others to make new friends.

★ Put social activities on a **calendar** so your loved one has things to look forward to enjoying.

An important thing to remember is that stamina may decrease as we age. Sometimes frequent, short visits and activities can be more beneficial than one long visit.

Realize that your loved one may no longer want to do a beloved activity after so many years (such as making food for a holiday, etc.). Respect this and ask how s/he might like to celebrate a special occasion nowadays. Perhaps your loved one prefers to be an observer instead of the host now. Try to be flexible, even it's a long-standing tradition.

★ If **transportation** or lack of motivation to do things is an issue, ask relatives and friends to accompany your loved one to the life-affirming activities from the list of social activities you made.

If there is no one able to accompany your loved one, hire a companion through a home care organization instead.

If your loved one is new to Uber/Lyft, a taxi, or public transportation, consider accompanying them for a time or two until they are comfortable with using it.

You may need to do research ahead of time if you have not taken public transportation recently.

There is GoGo Grandparent, which is easier to navigate for Uber/Lyft riders.

Research if your area is served by transport services for the elderly and the disabled called Paratransit and be sure to help with the enrollment process so that is not something your loved one puts off or uses as an excuse not to get out.

★ The benefits of **music** can't be overestimated. We know that music is a powerful way of engaging us, no matter what our physical or mental status. Play music and encourage singing and dancing often. Have fun making a list of favorite songs and podcasts that can be enjoyed. Create a reminder to put on music during a visit.

★ Don't forget about the **phone**. Ask family and friends to phone, daily calls can uplift and help maintain connection in an important way with others. Ask friends and family to invite your loved one to have a meal, run an errand or go for coffee together. Sometimes we need to be asked to do this if we have not heard from someone in a while.

★ It's okay to sit and watch favorite **movies** together. They can spark memories and stories so be willing to pause the movie to engage in talking.

★ Realize that increased interest in **religion** or a return to one's childhood religion is common as people age.

If this is of interest to your loved one, see what needs to be done to facilitate attending religious or spiritual services. Choose religious services that are held at quieter times of the week when congregations will be smaller, if needed.

Attend services with your loved one – or organize transport, if needed to attend the service. If needed, find out if a person from the faith community can do a home visit.

★ Having a reason to get up and out of the house can be a powerful deterrent to isolation. If your loved one wants to and is still able to **work**, help them identify work engagements that might be of interest, perhaps part-time instead of full-time. Employers can appreciate an older worker's knowledge, history, reliability, and customer service skills.

★ If they prefer to **volunteer**, help them seek those opportunities. Volunteering can make people feel better about themselves and their life. Steer them to places they can experience success. Realize that older adults can learn new technologies and skills but it may take them longer. Be sure to factor in transportation needed to get to work or volunteer assignments.

Chapter 8

Financial Matters

Financial Housekeeping

- See if your loved one will agree to reviewing their financial matters with you such as income sources, debts, monthly bills, etc.

- Do a review of insurance policies to determine if they are all still needed. Cancel or reduce coverage if not needed in order to free up some cash. This includes car insurance.

- It is possible to sell life insurance policies for cash. Check out one website for more details on mechanism for doing this: Rehburgsettlements.com.

- Check to see that property tax and home insurance have been paid on time.

- Put the due dates for all important bills to be paid on a calendar.

- Check to see that income tax has been filed for recent years or if a return needs to be filed.

- Assist in filing income tax return and paying income tax, especially if in arrears.

- Put the due date for filing the next income tax return on a calendar so loved one can be reminded.

Additional Sources of Help

Check to see if loved one was a member of any organization which offers benefits such as a fraternal organization (such as the Masons), a civic (Rotary), or religious organization. If a person qualifies, this income or the free services can help tremendously.

If your loved one has limited finances, consider calling local social service agencies to learn if additional forms of income or benefits could be applied for or if loved one could qualify for reduced fee services (phone, gas, electricity, rent, food, medication, health insurance, etc.)

When applying for low-income benefits, be prepared to spend time and energy following through on each step.

If assistance is needed with claims reimbursement for medical costs, contact the State Health Insurance Program for free assistance with Medicare claims. They can sit and go over Explanation of Benefit statements and help navigate reimbursement.

Scam Prevention

Financial elder abuse is a fast-growing crime and much of the abuse is happening online as well as perpetrated by family. Even the most intelligent, financially savvy people have been taken in by scams. Call the police or Adult Protective Services if you suspect any financial abuse. **If you sense that something isn't quite right, please do not hestitate to contact APS – they do not require physical proof to investigate.**

Reinforce that your loved one should never respond to anyone asking for personal information over the internet or on the telephone. Explain to your loved one that the best way to deter scammers is not to answer an unrecognized phone number in the first place! If they do answer, always hang up on callers that are fishing for personal information.

Explain to your loved one that online scams often try to scare people with a pop up like "your computer is infected with a virus, call this number to remove it immediately." Ask your loved one to call *you* if this happens, not the number on screen.

- If your loved one uses a computer, offer to monitor the history on a regular basis and delete phishing emails and fraudulent solicitations.

- Check the spam filter settings to try and reduce the number of junk emails.

- Purchase a service which can prevent a person from going on certain websites, like you might for a minor using the computer.

- It's getting harder to tell real mail from junk mail nowadays. Offer to go through the mail and throw away letters asking for money that are not the usual charities your loved one supports.

Legal Document

Just as all of us over 18 years old should have an Advance Health Care Directive, we also need a document that nominates someone to manage our financial affairs in the event we can't. That document is called a Financial Power of Attorney or Power of Attorney for Finances. The person you nominate in it is called your agent. Generally, a power of attorney form needs to be signed in front of a notary.

I suggest creating a <u>Durable</u> Power of Attorney because it remains in effect even if your parent becomes mentally incapacitated, e.g. gets dementia.

Typically, an attorney prepares a Financial Power of Attorney form for your parent to sign after discussing their specific wishes. This is done when they create estate planning documents such as a trust or will, and it's done at the same time they are nominating an agent to be their Power of Attorney for Health Care.

You don't have to use an attorney though. You can go online to download and print a document for your parent to complete.

Another way to help legally manage your parent's financial affairs is to go into the bank where your parent has an account and ask to sign *their* internal power of attorney form. This requires you to visit each financial institution because each bank uses its own forms. This bank's internal form will allow you, if you are made the agent, to manage affairs only at that particular bank.

With a Financial Power of Attorney in place, your parent can rest assured that if they're in a situation like a hospital or in rehab for a length of time, they have someone legally able to pay bills and take care of business matters until they can resume these tasks.

CAUTION: If you wait too long, your parent may lose the capacity to legally complete or sign the document due to mental changes such as dementia. You want to complete a form and have conversations well in advance and as health changes come up.

Once the form is completed, put a copy in the Legal section of the Reference Binder you made.

Financial transparency can be important in order to have family feel informed and comfortable. If you are the agent handling money matters, you may wish to offer a copy of monthly bank statements and financial records to other family. They can look at the statements and keep informed. Doing this also provides checks and balances, and you can answer any questions that come up along the way. You don't want your brother questioning you about an expense three years later.

If your parent does not wish to nominate a family member to handle financial affairs and act as their financial power of attorney, that's okay. They can hire a professional fiduciary who can become their power of attorney.

According to the California Department of Consumer Affairs, "Services provided by professional fiduciaries may include banking, paying bills, daily care, housing, tax preparation and payment, and household maintenance and upkeep. Some services, such as insurance and medical needs, real estate and personal property, and asset distribution, may be managed by the professional fiduciary themselves, or they may hire other professionals to perform those duties."

I have suggested that many clients hire a professional fiduciary. Since fiduciaries manage financial affairs as a profession, they are more efficient at it than most family members may be. Having that neutral, experienced professional can provide peace of mind to other family who may have differing ideas about how to manage a parent's estate. Also, it is one less area for you to be involved with. Again, if your parent agrees, the fiduciary can provide financial transparency to you and trusted others on a regular basis.

To find a professional fiduciary in your area visit: guardianship.org. For fiduciaries in California, fiduciary.ca.gov.

One area of financial risk I often see is when older adults have a home helper. The risk happens because your parent may ask *them* to go shopping and just hand them their debit card or cash. This can be risky. If your parent provides a debit card and there are thousands of dollars in the account, that opens up potential theft through large, unauthorized purchases. Most caregivers will do the right thing and head home with the items and correct change, but I've also known times when the helper purchases groceries for the client AND themselves with that cash or debit card, or gets cash OVER the purchase amount and pockets it during each shopping trip.

To reduce risk, it's a good idea to provide a limited amount gift card for the helper to shop with, or to get a TrueLink card for them to use instead.

A TrueLink card is a debit card customized for seniors. You load it with a specific amount and reload it as needed. This amount can be small, and spending is controlled this way. Visit Truelinkfinancial.com for more information on how this card works.

Read more about financial risks and mitigating them at AgingParents.com, a website and firm operated by colleagues who know this area well.

Chapter 9

Home Safety

A scary statistic: "Falls are the leading cause of fatal and non-fatal injuries for older Americans." (National Council on Aging)

FACTS ABOUT FALLING

- About one third of those over 65 fall each year, and the risk increases with age.

- Those who fall are two to three times more likely to fall again.

- 47% of people who fall and aren't injured cannot get up without assistance.

- Falls account for 25% of all hospital admissions and 40% of all nursing home admissions.

- The period of time elders who fall spend immobile often affects their health outcome. Muscle cell breakdown starts to occur within 30 to 60 minutes of compression due to falling. Dehydration, pressure sores, hypothermia, and pneumonia may result.

- 40% of those admitted to the hospital do not return to independent living; 25% die within a year.

To reduce fall risk, please conduct a household safety assessment. I use this tool with clients and invite you to use my form. It's not exhaustive but addresses some basics for reducing falls and accidents. While you are at it, look at your own home to reduce risks. It's never too early.

You may not be able to prevent your loved one's every fall, but spending the time to reduce risk is worth it. If they don't fall, you won't have to manage the journey through an emergency room, hospital, and rehab facility.

Once you reduce some of the risks, you'll rest easier and may alleviate some of the guilt if your parent does end up falling. Life is not perfect and there will always be risks. Being proactive will minimize accidents.

TIP: Do the household safety assessment in two parts. To avoid getting sidetracked, don't try to fix each problem as you take inventory.

Good news: At the end of this chapter you'll find ideas for addressing any problems you uncover.

Part 1

Walk through your parent's home, filling out the form as you go.

HOME SAFETY CHECKLIST

Yes/No   Pathways and hallways clear?

Yes/No   Walker or wheelchair fits through doorways and pathways easily?

Yes/No   Handrails on stairs inside home securely attached?

Yes/No   Adequate lighting in each room in daytime?

Yes/No   Adequate lighting at night?

Yes/No   Grab bars in shower?

Yes/No   Skid strips or textured mat on floor of shower/bathtub?

Yes/No   Grab bars by toilet?

Yes/No   Carpets in good repair? Note: Worn areas produce uneven surfaces, which cause falls.

Yes/No   Throw rugs attached securely so they don't move?

Yes/No   Cords or wires exposed that could cause tripping?

Yes/No   Can your parent easily care for pets?

Yes/No   Smoke detectors on each level of home working?

Yes/No   Fire extinguisher location known, nearby, and charged?

Yes/No   Is cooking area safe, with no flammable items near the burners?

Yes/No   Is there a telephone landline in case of emergency and if cell phones don't work?

Yes/No   Phone next to bed, in case of emergency?

Yes/No   Is phone easy to dial, with oversized numbers and back lighting?

Yes/No   Weapons in home? If so, are they loaded or unloaded?

Yes/No   Door and window locks working?

Yes/No   Secure handrails on stairs outside home?

Yes/No   Does parent have a medical alert system in case of emergency/accident/intruder?

Part 2

Review the form answers and think about where to make safety improvements. The sooner you do these, the better. Please don't wait until after the fall!

DAD NOTES: My dad parked his TV in the middle of his living room and ran the cord across the carpet, right in front of the kitchen. He told me the TV had to be there so he could have his sofa bed pulled out and the TV at his feet. If it had been against the wall, I guess he couldn't see or hear it too well. Drove me crazy with worry. I bought a mat and taped it down over the cord, so he and I wouldn't trip. It was not pretty, but he never fell, so it worked.

Who Does Needed Repairs?

Nonworking items, such as a fire extinguisher, a smoke alarm, or a burned-out light are easy fixes. So is picking up items from the floor so no one trips. Other fixes require a licensed contractor. Jump on all the easy stuff you can do then make a list for the contractor to do. Then set up an appointment to have those items addressed.

Some cities have programs that assist with home repairs, small and large. Call Eldercare Locator (800) 677-1116 to find out more or go to Eldercare. ACL.Gov.

Solutions to Reduce the Risk of Falls and Accidents

- If a walker or a wheelchair does not fit through a doorway, ask the contractor to rehang the door so there is more room. You can even make it swing in the opposite direction, or remove it altogether.

- Install railings on both sides of the steps.

- Put in brighter light bulbs where needed.

- Install night-lights. I suggest doing so near the bottom of a wall to illuminate paths when walking, especially from bed to bathroom. Try motion-sensor lights.

- Make it easier to care for pets: place the cat litter box on a higher surface so there's no bending over to clean it.

- Hire a dog walker, especially if the weather is cold, hot, or wet.

- Consider if you want to discuss removing weapons from the house. Elderly males, in particular, may use them for suicide, so removing them may be a good proactive measure.

- If a parent needs supervision getting in and out of bed, consider a wireless floor mat that signals an alarm in another room so you can be alerted to assist. Order from KerrMedical.com.

PHOTO COURTESY KERR MEDICAL DME INC.

- Throw rugs pose a big risk for falls because they may slip and slide. Ask permission to toss all throw rugs or put double-sided tape around the perimeters so that they stay in place. Or buy new rugs with better rubber backing. Consider the cost of a new rug vs cost of a new hip. For carpet runners and rugs with fringe, try to get permission to roll them up and store them.

- Have grab bars installed inside and outside shower area.

- Have grab bars installed next to toilet area. You would be surprised how many people use the towel rack for support and rip it out of the wall.

- To avoid tripping accidents, remove clutter. Pay close attention to items on closet floors.

- Repair broken or uneven steps inside and outside the home.

- You may want to buy something called a portable ramp for the front of the home or the garage stairway. This ramp folds out over the stairs so your loved one can get up a slope more easily. Single Fold Ramp from Spinlife.com. If you're concerned about looks or privacy, consider placing the ramp at a back entrance.

PHOTO COURTESY OF REVOLUTIONS INC.

- If you can persuade your parent not to get up on the step stool because you offer to do the ladder-type chores, go for it, if you feel comfortable.

- Put contrasting color tape on the edge of stairs inside the home so they are well delineated from each other since depth perception declines with age.

- Paint the outside step edges with a contrasting color to assist with depth perception decline. We painted three short horizontal strips of white paint on one particular step, which people tended to miss on our walkway. Now they notice that step.

- All states except New York and Washington, DC offer a program which provides a free phone with big buttons or other features that help those with diminished sight, hearing, or cognition. Call the Telephone Access Program (800) 806-1191 to get program information for your area.

While You're at It

- Purchase a waterproof mattress cover for the bed.

- If getting up and down from the couch is difficult, buy Assist-A-Tray. Manufactured by Stander, available from Parentgiving.com.

PHOTO COURTESY OF STANDER

If getting in and out of bed or turning is challenging, purchase under-the-mattress grab bars or a Bed Cane. Manufactured by Stander, available from Parentgiving.com, EZ Adjust Bed Rail or Bed Cane.

PHOTO COURTESY OF STANDER

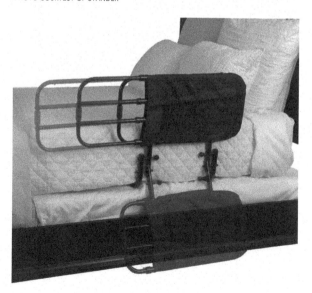

PHOTO COURTESY OF STANDER

If getting in and out of the car is difficult, buy a Swivel Seat Cushion – like a lazy Susan for your bottom. Also consider a Handy Bar that you can lean on when getting in and out of the car. Manufactured by Stander, available from Parentgiving.com.

PHOTO COURTESY OF STANDER

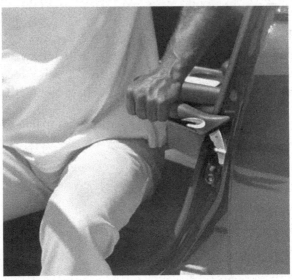

PHOTO COURTESY OF STANDER

Medical Alert and Personal Emergency Response Systems

I'm probably preaching to the choir and you're already worried that if your parent falls in their home it might take a while for someone to find them. Many older adults live alone, so when they fall it can be hours, or even days, before someone discovers them. It's really sad when clients tell me about their falls, how long they were on the ground, the pain they were in, how cold they were, and how afraid and helpless they felt.

Be that as it may, most of my older adult clients refuse a medical alert system. Families get very frustrated trying to talk their parent into getting one. I think older adults associate wearing a medical alert device with being old and they just don't see themselves as old or vulnerable. Refrain from pushing. What might have to happen is that your parent falls, THEN you reintroduce the idea and have success.

You can choose a company that offers a pendant or watch. Whenever your parent presses the button, they are connected to a response center for immediate assistance. Your parent can push the call button if fearful of an intruder, too.

Buttons are waterproof, so can be worn bathing, although many people take it off before bathing and then regret it because many falls happen in the bathroom.

AUTO ALERT: This feature means the pendant comes with an Auto Alert function and no one has to push the button. When the wearer falls, the fall is detected and help is immediately sent. This option is recommended for those who may forget to push the button or be reluctant to summon help.

To find a company, go online to see top rated companies under Personal Emergency Response or Medical Alert Systems.

A Safety Thought About Medications

Alcohol, medications, and over-the-counter meds can cause falls. Seemingly innocent medication, such as Advil PM, Benadryl, and many others, should be avoided in older adults.

Misuse of alcohol and drugs usually causes more issues as we age, and it doesn't resolve itself without help. If it's time to suggest professional treatment, consider speaking to a care manager or therapist about bringing up this important topic.

For more information on "Medications Older Adults Should Avoid or Use with Caution" go to HealthinAging.org.

Chapter 10

Care for Yourself

I realize that you're reading this book to help someone else, but I want to add ideas for looking out for yourself during this process also. If you're thinking of skipping this chapter, don't. Seriously. It's the most important chapter in this book.

The adage, "You must take care of yourself in order to be of use to others," is critical on Planet Eldercare.

The Heavy Grocery Bag Parable

You probably didn't plan on becoming a caregiver. You probably began doing it out of love and/or obligation, and soon it was all-consuming, part of what you do and who you are. It was probably gradual but now you may feel drained and not sure how to stop.

Let me illustrate: Say you meet a friend about to enter her house and she has a big bag of groceries in her arms. She asks you to hold the heavy bag for a minute while she gets out her keys to unlock her front door. You say, "Sure thing," and you wait while she digs out her keys. You would follow her inside and set the groceries down on her counter and leave.

BUT what if your friend took a year to find her keys and just left you standing there with the bag? Would you agree to that? Could you agree to that?

My point is that caregiving begins with agreeing to hold the bag for a minute or so but then it turns into this heavy thing you carry around. You have no idea how to put it down or even how to take some groceries out to lighten the bag. If you knew how long you'd be holding the bag, you would form a different, more realistic and sustainable plan.

 To see a video I did on caregiving where I call on an audience member to act out a skit about the grocery bag, go to https://youtu.be/jQpAg6GvNiw

Six Signs of Caregiver Fatigue and Burnout and Six Remedies

Sign #1: You want to run away and escape from everything!

I sure did. You are feeling crushed between handling both your own life and your parent's. Your unhealthy coping mechanisms may have increased; this is important to notice.

REMEDY: Go somewhere—the park, the movies, the mall, the gym. These activities are self-renewing and act as an immediate balm. I had to tell myself: put away the to-do list. Don't do one more errand. Stop, go play, recharge. You have permission, too.

If you're misusing a substance, this may be part of burnout, too. You need to address your use of alcohol, drugs, or painkillers. Talk to a professional counselor to evaluate how your behavior is linked to caregiving and how to reduce the pressure.

Sign #2: You notice your routine is off or you keep getting sick.

I could see my car needed servicing. I was eating unhealthy food late at night, and my exercise routine decreased. I gained 17 pounds in two years. These were all signs I was approaching caregiver burnout.

REMEDY: Book the oil change, doctor appointment, or nail appointment, mute your phone, or make a healthy meal. Get your own life in order. For each errand you run for your parent, do one for yourself. Keep the scales balanced. Remember, your life is important, too!

Sign #3: You begin to feel animosity toward your parent.
You say or do something mean, uncharacteristic, or unkind to the person you're caring for. Sometimes verbal and physical abuse occurs.

REMEDY: Do less. Get off the merry-go-round. Do something that restores you to your more balanced self. It may be time to attend a support group or individual therapy to cope with caregiver burden.

In addition to feeling resentful of the *time* you're spending you may notice all the *money* you're spending on their behalf also. Buying incidental expenses for another can add up quickly.

REMEDY: Arrange to meet with family members to discuss how your out-of-pocket costs might be split, if not reimbursed by your loved one.

Keep track of the time that you spend on caregiving – that will help you determine whether some tasks might better be delegated to others within the family or to hired help.

REMEMBER: It's acceptable to be reimbursed for your time and expenses so you don't leave yourself without enough money when you're older yourself!

DAD NOTES: I got mad one afternoon when my dad questioned the brand of an over-the-counter medication I bought for him, which he asked for. It was the end of a long day and I lost it. I just threw down some paperwork I brought over, left the medication on the table, and angrily walked out. I didn't need this crap. Enough is enough. I was not feeling appreciated and it was the last straw.

Sign #4: You avoid socializing.

REMEDY: Reluctance to go out with friends might mean you're nesting and rebuilding. That can be a good thing but it's also important to hang out with your friends. Take the first step and give a friend a call. It really can ease caregiving stress.

DAD NOTES: I feel as though each evening something goes wrong with Dad. I went home Wednesday night and just watched So You Think You Can Dance on TV and talked with my housemate. He noticed I was sad and heavy at first but better as the night wore on. I think just having a normal routine for a few hours, like I used to—my own rather than Dad's—was healthy. Need to tell people how important getting back in touch with normalness is to their being able to cope.

Sign #5: You have dark thoughts you're afraid to mention.

You may want to drop your Dad off at the Emergency Room and keep driving into the sunset. This actually has a name, "Pop Drop." This happens when family is completely overwhelmed and feels they have no other choices and can't take the stress of caring for the person any more.

Maybe you secretly hope your loved one dies or moves away, and you really don't care where. Contemplating the death of your parent is completely normal. I hear this regularly from clients, and I felt this despair myself. When my dad would go away, I sometimes wondered if he never returned, how would I feel? When I was overwhelmed, I figured this was good—less work for me. Other times I would cry, thinking how awful it was that I would have that thought.

These thoughts are part of caregiver burnout. You are now doing too much caring and worrying. This also may mean you lack proper support.

REMEDY: You have to get help. Friends usually want to help but aren't sure what you need. When someone asks what they can do to help, be prepared with an answer. Make a list of tasks you do. Maybe they can do the shopping or drive Mom to an event. Maybe you can ask them to do a chore you need done for you, while you tend to Mom.

This also signals that you need to take time off in some way—a vacation, a staycation, or even asking someone to step in so you don't need to see Dad for a while. My sister came into the picture big time when I got angry with my father and walked out of his apartment. Thanks, Sis.

I have this offbeat idea: what if we all switched parents? Maybe your friend takes your mom to lunch and you take hers? I believe it would be good for everyone. You hear someone's stories for the first time and parents get an attentive listener. Maybe that could morph into taking each other's parents to the store to shop? Maybe you would have more patience with your friend's mom than your own.

Sign #6: You avoid answering your phone or checking email.

The phone rings. You see it's your loved one, and you roll your eyes and think, "What now?" You don't answer, but then you feel guilty. You worry that it might be an emergency and you've let your parent down. At the same time, you know that if you pick up that phone you're going to explode.

DAD NOTES: Dad called me at five o'clock on a Saturday morning from the emergency room and asked me to bring him some cough drops! I told him, "Are you kidding? No, sorry, I'm asleep. I'm sure you can ask a nurse for one." and I went back to sleep.

REMEDY: Let the call go to voicemail and check the message when you're in a better frame of mind; most likely, the information can wait. If it's a true emergency, your parent can push the button on the medical alert system or call 911.

Sometimes it's all a matter of perspective.

DAD NOTES: One day after Dad's radiation treatment, I was driving him back home. He was frail and complaining. His cell phone rang, and suddenly his demeanor changed. He was positive and upbeat. I felt I was driving with Dr. Jekyll and Mr. Hyde. I thought, Oh, I see. You're all sunshine and light with your buddy while I'm stuck with all the work and complaining. Grumble, grumble.

Upon reflection, it was a good thing to listen to the way he related his condition to another. He wanted others to believe he was doing well. I realize, too, that he could be himself with me. He didn't need to pretend things were easy if they were not. I consider it a gift that I got to hear his authentic feelings.

When Do We Learn to Connect to Ourselves?

Is it when we reach a certain age? Is it modeled for us?

Is it after a diagnosis of disease or is it never?

When will you start to take care of yourself if you are not doing that now and what will motivate you? How can you do it?

One doctor wrote prescriptions to caregivers, such as, "Don't visit your parent this weekend." Or, "Take one-week vacation." This empowered the caregivers since it was the doctor's orders and official. You should not expect yourself to work seven days a week and not take a break. Self-renewal doesn't have to cost anything nor take a lot of time.

Parents may not see all you are doing, and they may not appreciate that you're doing so much. They may not know the impact their care is having on you. They are looking at life from a changed perspective, and it may be a slightly selfish one at this point, or they may be unaware due to memory loss. When they're ailing, they're not in the best shape to parent you, which, secretly, you may still want.

You have to give yourself permission to take breaks for play and relaxation. When you take a few days off, you'll feel better, and your parent may appreciate you even more when you return.

I witness the strain of caregiving on client families daily. It can take a toll on health and lifespan. Please reduce your load so you can remain healthy. I have seen caregivers become ill and die and their parents go on living for years.

DAD NOTES: I went to a business meeting after my father died, one that I normally attended but had not been to for several months. People came over and said I looked great – new haircut and lipstick. One woman asked if I had been on vacation. Interesting. My dad died, and I began to attend to my own needs again, so my face relaxed. I was no longer taking care of two lives.

Activities Just for You

Do something you love. Rediscover what inspires and recharges you.

- Paint, draw, or color
- Hike
- Watch uninterrupted TV
- Play with your pet
- Garden
- Go to the library
- Listen to music
- Lie in the grass or on the beach
- Window shop
- Go to a park and watch little kids
- Read
- Take a nap
- Stretch
- Dance
- Call a friend and make a date to meet
- Swim
- Play a board game or cards

Chapter 11

Doctor Appointments

It's wise to form a rapport with your parent's physicians before issues become serious, if possible. These relationships can be even more vital when you are dealing with a loved one who has memory issues. You may be the one calling to check on lab results or medication refills when your parent isn't up to it. When you attend an appointment, the physician sees you as a source of support and information. This physician is more likely to chat with you by phone when a crisis arises. You want this connection—and so does the doctor.

First Doctor Visit

If there is confidential information about your parent that you think the physician needs ahead of time (a particular concern you wish to address), write it down and provide it to the receptionist when you arrive or fax or email the information before you go.

You are free to tell the doctor your concerns but realize that he or she would need authorization from the patient before responding to your questions.

Each doctor's office has a HIPAA form you can fill out and your parent can sign, authorizing communication between you and the doctor about your parent. Once your parent signs the form it's part of the office record. Ask for a copy to place in your Reference Binder. If your parent refuses to sign the form, revisit the issue at another time.

If your parent hasn't done so already, bring a copy of the advance health care directive and give it to the receptionist to put in your parent's medical file.

During the first doctor visit with your parent, I recommend being a quiet observer. If you dominate, you may appear disrespectful or overbearing. Instead, observe the interaction between your parent and the doctor.

Offer to excuse yourself at some point so your parent and the physician can interact privately.

Ask the doctor for a list of diagnoses and medications. Place copies in your Reference Binder. You may want to compare the doctor's medication list with the one you made in Chapter 4 to see if there are discrepancies.

These lists will be of great value if your parent goes to the emergency department.

Take notes at the doctor's appointment to review with your parent later. It's easy to miss instructions or fail to absorb all that the doctor covers.

DAD NOTES: 1/30 Went to Dr. Hsu (oncologist). Watching for low blood count, as this is sign of lymph worsening. Does not see any indication of this, so no reason to think lymph aggressive.

Spot under arm now palpable, was not before. About two fingers in width. Labs look good now; doctor wants LDH measured today (we went to lab for draw; low before—78 now). Good news. LDH is enzyme in cells; when tumors are active, they break apart. We might see high numbers if lymphoma worsening. If node gets bigger, we can decide then to take out node in general surgery; he'd do bone-marrow biopsy at hips (local, not general anesthetic).

Renewed Lisinopril for us; hope will mail

NOTE: I took these notes during the appointment and they may not be accurate, but this is what I understood at the time.

Second Doctor Visit

Now that you have met the doctor, you may want to ask questions to get a better handle on your parent's health condition. How do you go about this? Each loved one is different.

Option 1) If there are specific questions that need answers, share them with your parent and encourage them to ask the doctor. This will empower them and they are the patient, after all.

Option 2) Some parents appreciate your asking the questions, it shows your concern. They feel your support and it reinforces your relationship with them. Others may be too ill or have memory loss and may be unable to track the conversation or ask questions. Make sure you ask permission from your parent, though, before you speak directly to the doctor, to show respect.

Pack up all of your parent's meds and supplements to take to this visit or bring the medication list you made earlier in Chapter 4. Now is the time to discuss any discrepancies you noticed so an accurate list can be recorded.

Ask the doctor if any medications can be discontinued. With fewer meds, your parent saves money and there's less time getting medications refilled. Get permission from your parent before requesting changes, though, since some people are very married to the meds they take.

Chapter 12

Hospital Visit Preparations

If your parent goes into the hospital, it may be unplanned. Take some time to read over and answer the following questions so all are better prepared.

Before a Hospital Stay

- Give a trusted person a spare key to home

- Have cash on hand to provide to someone who can buy groceries or meds or needed equipment

- Ask someone to be an advocate, available to speak with hospital staff

- Consider who will care for pets

- Consider whether or not parent is comfortable with people visiting them while in the hospital

- Complete an advance health care directive and go over health care wishes with agent

While in Hospital, Arrange for Someone to

- Pay bills

- Water houseplants and garden

- Take care of pets

- Bring in mail and newspapers

- Look at calendar and cancel appointments

- Check e-mail/voicemail, if needed

- Empty house garbage and put out trash

- Clean out refrigerator of spoiling foods

- Wash dishes and tidy house

Prior to Coming Home from the Hospital, Arrange for Someone to

- Shop for food

- Prepare some meals

- Change bed linens

- Stay the first night or more

- Decide if parent wants visitors at home and how soon; appoint one person to explain situation to friends, if needed

- Ask clergy to visit, if desired

- Ask someone to make hair/nail care appointment (to come to the home, if needed)

List compiled by Kira Reginato on behalf of American Society on Aging conference members, September, 2009

Chapter 13

Grab and Go Bag

To ensure maximum readiness for hospital and emergency room visits, create a Grab and Go Bag as soon as possible. It consists of two parts:

1. **A Hospital Binder**
   Vital information staff may need at the hospital.

2. **Personal Items**
   Allow an hour or two to create and assemble items for the binder and another thirty minutes to gather personal items into a backpack or suitcase.

Part One – Assemble Hospital Binder

Get out the remaining materials you used to create the Reference Binder in Chapter 5.

1. **Create a cover sheet for front of binder that says:**
   Information for Hospital

   Patient Name: _____

2. **Label a divider PATIENT INFO**

3. **Complete the Patient Info form on the following page**
   This demographic info is commonly referred to as a "face sheet" in the health care industry. Place it in the binder.

PATIENT INFORMATION FORM

Patient Name: _____

Date of Birth: _____

Address: _____

City/State/Zip: _____

Cell Phone: _____

Home Phone: _____

Medicare #: _____

Supplemental Health Insurance: _____

Medical Record #: _____

Social Security #: _____

Veteran's #: _____

Primary Care Doctor Name: _____

Address: _____

City/State/Zip: _____

Phone: _____

Fax: _____

EMERGENCY CONTACTS:
(Indicate if anyone is the legal agent for making health care decisions,
Power of Attorney for Health Care)

Name/Relationship: _____

Cell: _____

Work: _____

Name/Relationship: _____

Cell: _____

Work: _____

Long-Term Care Insurance Company: _____

Policy ID Number: _____

Address: _____

City/State/Zip: _____

Phone: _____

Fax: _____

Long-Term Care Insurance covers:

Home Care (Nonmedical)? _____

Assisted Living? _____

Skilled Nursing Care? _____

Maximum amount paid per month by long-term care insurance: $ _____

_____

4. **Label a divider HEALTH INSURANCE**
Make a copy of all health insurance cards, both front and back. Put these copies in a plastic sheet and place in binder.

5. **Label the next divider MEDICATION**
Insert a copy of the current, reconciled medication list.

6. **Label another divider DIAGNOSES**
Insert the list you got from your parent's doctor.

7. **Label a divider DIRECTIVES**
Insert a copy of the completed advance health care directive form. This document gives you, or the designated agent, the right to make medical decisions for your parent, if he/she is incapable. Hospital staff may want to see a copy of this document.

Unsightly as it may seem, it's common for older adults to post their advance health care directive on the refrigerator because EMTs are trained to look for it there.

IF your parent has a POLST (Physician Orders for Life-Sustaining Treatment) form or a DNR (Do Not Resuscitate) form:

Place a copy of the brightly-colored POLST form at the front of the binder. Leave the original form on the refrigerator, where emergency help will see it.

Place a copy of the DNR form at the front of the binder. Leave the original form on the refrigerator, where emergency help will see it.

You may wish to take a picture of these forms with your phone so that you have mobile access to the data at any time.

8. **Insert blank sheets of binder paper**
You can use these to take notes when you are at the doctor's office, the hospital or emergency room.

9. **Make a copy of all you included in this Hospital Binder and put it into the Reference Binder you already made**

Part Two – Pack Personal Items

Find a backpack or suitcase to hold the Hospital Binder, and then add these essentials:

- ☐ Robe and slippers (put your parent's name on them)

- ☐ Comfortable clothes and pair of shoes to wear home

- ☐ Spare eyeglasses

- ☐ Hairbrush, comb, toothbrush, toothpaste, razor, deodorant

- ☐ Book/magazine

- ☐ Note pad and pen

- ☐ Change for vending machines
  (Dad wanted the newspaper and candy)

- ☐ Phone charger, if needed

- ☐ Mirror, makeup, if desired

- ☐ _____

- ☐ _____

- ☐ _____

- ☐ _____

Congratulations, the Grab and Go Bag is now complete. When the time comes to take your parent for medical treatment, you will feel prepared and more confident. The medical staff will be very appreciative of this helpful information at their fingertips.

Decide where to put the Grab and Go Bag. Tell family and caregivers where they can find the bag, to be given to the emergency medical staff when they arrive or for you to get before heading to the hospital. Consider putting a note on the refrigerator for the EMTs, giving the location of the Grab and Go Bag.

Chapter 14

Emergency Room Visits

There is typically a long wait to be seen in an Emergency Room, now called the Emergency Department. If you want to avoid "waiting in chairs," then you need to call an ambulance. The medical staff will give your parent preferential treatment and attend to him or her sooner if brought in by ambulance.

At the Emergency Department

Bring the Grab and Go Bag you already packed. Look at how prepared you are. Good job! If you have time, you can also print out a few pages of recent history from the computer file you started in Chapter 3.

Take this book along so you can read tips while you are there.

If you are your parent's advocate, be prepared to share some of the contents of the Hospital Binder with the medical staff. They may appreciate having a copy of the face sheet of general info, health insurance cards, the advance health care directive, and medication list.

Be prepared to give a brief history to the doctor, unless your parent is willing and able. Remember it's empowering for your parent to speak for themselves. If they are getting off course or inaccurate, politely ask your parent "Do you mind if I tell the doctor about why we're here today?"

How to Advocate and Care for Your Parent in the Emergency Department

If it's been hours since your parent has had food or water, ask staff if your parent may eat or drink. Your parent may not be allowed to eat or drink if surgery or tests are pending but if not, staff can have a tray of food delivered. This is a good time for you to leave and eat healthy food, too.

Ask if you can dim the light so your parent can close their eyes. Rest, even for a short time, is important for both of you.

While waiting, get out music/podcasts and ear buds so your loved one can listen.

While you're waiting, write down what medical tests are being done, their results, what the doctor tells you, and any questions you can think of. Use the blank paper in the Hospital Binder.

Ask for comfort items you think will help, such as a heated blanket, socks, or extra pillows. The hospital staff is busy, so they may not offer, but they do care that your loved one is comfortable.

If you and your loved one are getting bored, consider using this time to have your loved one tell you about old times or relatives. You can take some notes or even record on your phone and have some living history documented. Oral history is a wonderful gift and capturing some of it now can take your mind off things.

How to Care for Yourself at the Emergency Department

Yes, that's right, you must care for yourself in the ED, too. You may be there for hours.

Ask staff to estimate how long things will take so you can leave for a while, but remain nearby. Try not to feel guilty about leaving; your loved one is being cared for. Get some fresh air.

DAD NOTES: At the VA, I had a hard time coping. Overstimulated, I think. Nowhere to have a quiet conversation or not see so many people. Went to my car and worked about ninety minutes and felt better. I need to remember this. Later went and parked by the beach to unwind. Being away from hospital helps.

Give your phone number to staff so they can call you when an issue comes up or discharge is imminent.

Call one relative with an update. Ask if they will phone others for you. Remember, you can call people later and update them. Things may change a lot in the next few hours, so if you try to keep everyone updated with the latest, you could make yourself nutty.

Don't expect to do any office work at the ED; multi-tasking leads to frustration. It was better for me to leaf through a magazine or read a book when I got bored.

Eat fruits and vegetables and drink lots of water.

As much as you can, document all that is going on so you can update your computer file. Over the years, your parent may go through many tests and hospital stays. It's difficult to keep track of all the medical information. They won't recall it all, and neither will you after a while. If you write it down as you go, you can look back and easily get the facts.

Take the time to confide your feelings to an understanding friend or a diary. This entry is from one of my dad's ED visits; it was a relief to vent.

DAD NOTES: I feel alone here, like I have no support system. This is a roller coaster of Dad's being well then crashing. In the ED, no one tells you how long you will be there, you wait for hours, unable to move, get work done. Fragmented day, fluorescent lights, awful!

For more advice on how to deal with your own stress level and find some peace, go to Chapter 10.

Chapter 15

Hospital Discharge

I've found that the hospital discharge day is a busy and stressful time. It's very easy for oversights to occur, which can actually lead to another hospital stay. Take the time to get complete instructions before you leave the hospital.

Refer to the "Hospital Discharge Checklist" in this chapter.

The staff member helping with the discharge can go by several names: social worker, discharge planner, case manager, or nurse. For our purposes, we'll use the term "discharge planner" (DP).

Here's what should happen: The discharge process begins shortly after your loved one is admitted to the hospital. The DP should ask how things are at home and explain the anticipated discharge plan, subject to change, of course. If a staff member doesn't approach you, approach them about a plan as soon as possible after arrival. They should be willing to hear your thoughts and work to address concerns.

Too often the family gets a call from the discharge planner saying, "Your dad is going home tomorrow." You panic, especially if you're worried that he doesn't have what he needs at home or can't return home.

A hospital staff member may try to discharge your loved one before there is a thought-out, coordinated, safe plan in place. You have the right to push back by saying, "You can't discharge my dad today. It's not safe for him to go home yet." You may need time to get grab bars or handrails installed. You may need to hire in-home help, or you may need to find an assisted living community that will welcome your parent with open arms. If it is not safe for him to go home yet, speak up! Those assertive words should give you some much-needed time to put care into place.

Day of Discharge

On discharge day, the DP comes to the room to give instructions for going home.

Your parent may be like my clients and my dad. They are so preoccupied with putting on clothes and gathering things that they don't hear the instructions. Try to be there and listen closely to help prevent errors that could lead to readmission.

DAD NOTES: I remember my father hollering at the DP. She was going over the home instructions and needed him to sign the release form. He said, "No! I'm not signing anything. I'm going home to die!" It was embarrassing for me—and heartbreaking, too. He wasn't accurate. He lived a long time after that, but at that moment he was upset.

The DP provides written discharge instructions. Even if they are not fully digestible now, read them over. You will learn what is expected to be done after the hospital stay to aid your parent's recovery. Put them in your Reference Binder.

Follow-Up Appointments

Ask about the schedule for follow-up appointments or tests. These are typically listed in the discharge instructions.

Remember: Geriatric care managers, like me, can help you through this transition time. We act as patient and family advocates. We can be there on discharge day to read the discharge instructions and to try to minimize communication breakdowns during the transition back home. See Chapter 2 for more on care managers.

Hospital Discharge Checklist

Use this checklist early and often during your loved one's hospitalization. Skip what doesn't apply.

Date of Admission to Hospital: _____

Reason for Admission: _____

_____

Discharge Planner Name: _____

Discharge Planner Phone: _____

Planned Date for Leaving Hospital: _____

Equipment and Safety

- **What equipment will be needed at home?** (e.g., a wheelchair, walker, hospital bed, or bedside commode) _____

_____

_____

_____

- **Does your parent have any of this equipment at home in good working order?** If so, let discharge planner know. _____

_____

_____

- **Will Medicare cover cost of equipment?** If not, will supplemental insurance cover costs? If not, what is the out-of-pocket cost? _____

_____

_____

- **Name and phone number of company delivering medical equipment?** _____

  _____

  _____

  When will equipment be delivered? _____

- **Is oxygen being delivered? Name and phone number of supplier:** __

  _____

  _____

  When will oxygen be delivered? _____

Give your schedule so you can be there.

What if Medicare or insurance doesn't cover needed equipment? In my town we have a medical equipment recycling program. Many communities have a similar place, run by volunteers, that collects and distributes shower chairs, wheelchairs, lift chairs, canes, and even unopened boxes of undergarments. You can pick up what you need and donate what you don't use. Find out if your community has any type of recycling program or look online for used medical equipment.

What will patient need help with at home?

- ☐ Bathing
- ☐ Dressing
- ☐ Toileting
- ☐ Walking
- ☐ Eating
- ☐ Transferring from the bed to a chair
- ☐ Transportation

☐ Bill paying

☐ Medication

☐ Climbing stairs

☐ Cooking

☐ Help at night

☐ Wound care

☐ Injections

☐ _____

☐ _____

Aftercare and Training

☐ Arrange for the discharge plan to be explained when the whole family can be present with the patient. Invite any person you are hiring to help at home to hear the plan also.

Family often incorrectly assumes that any care needed at home after a hospital stay will be covered by insurance. If your loved one needs a skilled professional to do nursing care, physical therapy, speech therapy, or occupational therapy, the doctor can order home health care.

☐ Will there be home health care ordered by the doctor?

Home health care company contact info: _____

_____

☐ Will the patient need ongoing home care not covered by insurances? If your loved one doesn't qualify for home health care services, you have to pay for help from a home care organization or do it yourself. This is nonmedical help. What a difference one word makes: home care versus home *health* care.

☐ If you want home help, ask the discharge planner to arrange a meeting with a private-pay, nonmedical home care organization while your parent is still in the hospital. This way paperwork can be signed prior to going home.

Name of home care organizations provided and contact info: _____

_____

_____

_____

_____

☐ Ask for any training needed from staff before discharge.

This can include safe movement, getting in and out of a car, using a spirometer, negotiating stairs, and so forth.

Ask if a physical therapist can show family or hired caregivers how to safely transfer and move the patient. You want all the people involved in your parent's care to know how to care for your loved one and themselves, safely. Using correct body mechanics is crucial. Feel free to ask for written directions.

☐ What signs and symptoms should you be concerned about if you see them at home? When should you call the doctor or return to the hospital? _____

_____

_____

_____

_____

_____

_____

Medication

☐ Ask to see the full list of medications at discharge.

☐ With your parent present, ask a hospital staff member about instructions for any new meds—and any possible side effects. If there's no time to do this, ask the pharmacist.

☐ Take a look at the medication list you made at home. How do the lists compare? Is there a new medication? Has a medication been discontinued or a dose changed? Try to reconcile any differences and ask questions while your parent is still in the hospital.

☐ Communicate with discharge planner about the specific pharmacy to fill any prescriptions, unless you will be using the hospital pharmacy.

☐ Pick up prescriptions before you get your loved one ready to leave the hospital.

Transportation

Ask discharge planner about transportation to next location. Staff may expect you to drive your parent home unless told otherwise. However, you are under no obligation to drive them.

Your parent will be weak from the hospital stay, and safety is important for both of you. You don't want to hurt yourself or take on more than you can handle, so feel free to say no.

If you don't want to drive your parent home, ask the discharge planner to make other arrangements. If your parent needs to go home in a wheelchair, the DP may arrange for nonemergency wheelchair transport. The transport company driver will wheel your loved one out of the hospital, drive them home, and wheel them off the van into the home. Your loved one or you will need to pay for this service.

☐ Confirm transport date and time: _____

_____

☐ By ambulance: _____

☐ By private transport company: _____

☐ By family: _____

☐ Confirm location to be transported: _____

_____

_____

_____

Chapter 16

Home from the Hospital

Your parent is out of the hospital, now what? Well, if they are back at home, that may become a very busy place.

In the hospital, patient activities are scheduled and there are professionals at all hours. All that changes when your parent returns home. There's a lot for the parent and the family to manage. Many family caregivers have no training or experience; people just figure it out as they go along.

Let's map out how to coordinate this kind of effort.

As soon as your parent is home, read the hospital discharge instructions. Follow them carefully and call the doctor's office with any questions.

Add the date of the hospitalization to the top of the computer file you started in Chapter 3, for easy reference.

Create an online calendar for others to view such as LotsaHelpingHands. com or CaringBridge.org. Here you can post what you need help with: transportation, shopping, errands, laundry, and so forth. People with permission to view the calendar can sign up to do a task. That makes your life easier: there are no phone calls to make and people choose what they feel comfortable doing.

Schedule a family meeting or call. If you don't have siblings, are there other family members who might be willing to assist in taking care of your loved one? If so, ask if they might be willing to talk through the tasks that are ahead and offer ways they might contribute.

Have family members complete the Support System Questionnaire in Chapter 1, if they haven't already. This will help inform everyone what professional services need to be paid versus what the family will handle.

Be realistic during the meeting with your family. Is it reasonable to ask your sister to help manage your parent's finances at this time if she can't manage her own? Or, if your brother is a big-picture thinker, why ask him to do detail work, like setting up medications? Honor each other's skills and divvy up responsibilities accordingly.

I suggest you train your parents on what they can and can't expect from you, in terms of caring for them. The sooner you do this, the better.

Follow-Up Appointments

Get a large calendar and keep it centrally located in your parent's home where all can see it.

Mark each appointment on the calendar, whether a person is coming to see your Mom or if she has an appointment out. Seeing commitments on a calendar gives structure to the day.

If you have not been able to take your parent to a doctor's appointment yet, offer to go to the follow-up one after the hospital stay.

Be sure to arrange transportation to appointments. You may want to call the nonemergency medical transport company that brought your parent home from the hospital. There may be a van service for disabled people that offers transportation. You can meet at the appointment if you will not be driving your parent.

DAD NOTES: I prefer to be earning money on a workday rather than being at the VA all day so I decided to make Dad's appointments in the afternoon. That way I can at least work in the morning, when I'm most productive. Can't get much done on computer in waiting rooms with multiple interruptions. Or I can get my daughter or another to drive him to appointments.

Movement

Hospitals are notorious for having people stay in bed way too much. Don't get me started. We are not made for staying in bed 22 to 24 hours a day!

While patients are in the hospital, they lose muscle strength. Here's a sobering figure that I tell clients: experts estimate that for each day we are in the hospital, it takes three to seven days to regain our baseline strength. So, if your loved one was in the hospital for seven days, it will be 21 to 49 days until they are back to their own version of normal.

Encourage movement once your parent is home, unless doctor's orders say otherwise. Walk, walk, and walk some more, outside if possible.

The added benefits of getting outside are deeper breathing, sunshine, vitamin D for stronger bones, and a rise in serotonin for combating depression. They will see, hear, and smell the outside world, which is good for their brain and good for their emotional and psychological health. If you walk with them, you both benefit.

If walking is not an option, consider doing range-of-motion limb exercises daily. Look online for a tutorial that makes sense.

Mark the calendar each time your loved one exercises. This will keep them accountable. Plus, everyone can track progress and compliment the effort or consistency.

DAD NOTES: *When my dad was spending too much time indoors during his cancer treatments, I suggested that he walk or sit in the sun. He jumped on that idea and went outside with the paper daily, actually getting a tan from sitting on the balcony. I'd come up the stairs of his apartment building and find him outside, shirt off, reading happily, and looking content, soaking up some sun. Initially, he was really weak and short of breath and could barely walk outside his apartment. But with time and effort, he prided himself on ambling around the perimeter of his apartment building on the second floor. He increased his stamina until he was able to go downstairs and get his mail. He took joy in regaining his strength, and he loved measuring his progress and reporting it to me.*

Promoting Independence

To allow independent dressing to continue, provide pull-on pants, slip-on shoes and specialty items such as a button aid, zipper pull, or sock aid available at a medical supply store or online.

Be aware that needing assistance with dressing, bathing, moving from bed to chair, or using the toilet can be triggers for qualifying to use a long-term care insurance policy.

If your loved one will no longer drive, apply for a handicapped placard so you can use parking spaces close to shopping and doctors when out with them.

Incontinence

Not getting to the toilet in time may be due to several factors. The brain might not get the signal to use the toilet soon enough or your loved one may have trouble getting up or walk too slowly to get to the toilet in time.

Sometimes people are constipated and when they take a laxative, can't get to the toilet in time. No matter the cause, it can be embarrassing and oftentimes a person will not leave the house if the problem gets severe or the person lives in fear of having an accident.

• We want people to have an active life and go out as often as they wish.

• Make an appointment with a doctor to assess possible causes and remedies for continence problems. Females may benefit from an appointment with a uro-gynecological doctor.

• Provide additional toilet facilities such as a commode or urinal in the room. Provide incontinence aids such as disposable undergarments and pads.

• Act on signs that your loved one needs to use the toilet and assist them immediately.

• Provide easy-to-remove clothing such as pull-on pants. Avoid zippers or buttons.

- Limit fluid intake prior to sleep but avoid the temptation to limit fluids in the day. Dehydration leads to more problems than incontinence.

- Put a waterproof pad on the bed, couch, chairs, and car seat.

- Provide regular two-hour reminders to use toilet.

- Be aware that incontinence can be a trigger for qualifying to use a long-term care insurance policy.

Communication

Consider getting an adaptive phone with enlarged buttons, picture squares, flashing light for incoming calls, etc., depending on what issue is causing the difficulty in using the phone.

- Provide written instructions about how to retrieve messages.

- Ask if it is okay to check messages left on phone when you visit.

- Consider changing the outgoing message on the telephone to include an alternative number to call, such as yours.

- If loved one can't use a phone without assistance, consider employing a caregiver because this signals a person who should probably not be living alone.

- If it is a challenge to dial, ensure that there is another means of calling for assistance such as a Personal Emergency Response System.

- Check and adjust telephone ringer volume or add amplified ringer, if needed.

- Consider a phone like Raz Memory Cell Phone, which is very simple to operate and allows access only from callers that you have put on the face of the phone, RazMobility.com.

Medication Management

Helping your parent stay on top of meds can be a big job, so budget enough time to handle this task.

If you haven't done this already, now is a good time to read Chapter 4 to learn tools for managing medication regimens.

Engagement

We all need a reason to get up each day. What we have to do shapes our day and our lives.

When people are stuck at home, they can get cabin fever. Without tasks to accomplish or a reason to get up, depression, boredom, and loneliness can set in.

Encourage your parent to dress in street clothing and do basic grooming every day, to the extent that they can. If needed, try an electric toothbrush which requires less hand dexterity for keeping teeth and gums healthy.

Consider what your parent enjoys and create a regular "job" around it. We all need to be needed.

DAD NOTES: Here's what I did to help get my dad out of the house. I asked him to get my mail at the PO Box. I asked him to drive me home when I dropped off my car to be repaired. I asked him to come over, set up the poker table, and teach some friends how to play. I also asked his advice for home repairs and borrowed his tools. When Dad developed an interest in cooking, I asked him to make me dinner, so he could try out his new recipes. We ate together often. He also played the stock market with my sister. They talked daily about how the market was doing, and he learned to use an iPad and use E-Trade Financial. And, amazingly, he played online chess with a young friend—all this technical prowess from a man who needed a year to figure out how to use his cell phone. Where there is interest, there is engagement!

Chores

Be alert to what daily chores need to be done. Show up consistently to handle the tasks you agreed to handle, so your parent can depend on that, but only help until your parent can resume doing them. It is not healthy to prolong their dependency.

Check out this phrase: "learned helplessness." Professionals use it to describe what can happen when you do too much for someone, helping beyond what is currently needed. We see this often in institutions.

Older people get used to letting us do things for them and then learn to be helpless. Let Mom or Dad do whatever part of a task they can, no matter how long it takes. Back off as they regain their strength and confidence. Remember their need for engagement.

How to Keep Your Caregiving Manageable

To arrive home with energy and sanity from going out, my golden rule is to go with your parent on only ONE errand/outing per day. I know the bank may be near the pharmacy, but going to both in one day is often too much. Just do one task, and then head home with your parent. You may be thinking, "What? That's not efficient!" You're right. It pains me to do only one thing, too. In the long run, you will both arrive home less stressed. Go at their pace, not yours.

Ask your parent to keep a shopping list. Encourage them to go with you to the store. This activity and use of energy will help them sleep better. If they refuse to go out with you, do yourself a favor and schedule shopping only once a week.

Often the daily request for an item from the store is code for I'm lonely. You know they're not going to perish if they don't have shampoo, but they can make it seem urgent, can't they?

DAD NOTES: I told Dad I'm only shopping Wednesday and Saturday for him. And on Wednesday I called and got his list. He was ready. He and my daughter made fun of me. He said, "Yeah, I guess your mom doesn't want to shop every day." (No kidding, Dad).

Chapter 17

Refusing Paid Help

Your parent is home and you've been helping a lot, so what now? Well, you can continue helping forever. Seriously, some do this without even realizing it. But you probably can't – and shouldn't – keep living their life and yours forever.

You may be interested in hiring some help but you've already tried having that conversation with your parent and it didn't go well. Right? I didn't just read your mind. It's rare for a loved one to agree to hired help, for obvious and not so obvious reasons.

Before bringing up the subject again, close your eyes and imagine that you are the one needing help. Change places with your loved one for a minute. How would you want others to approach you if you were no longer able to care for yourself independently? How would you want someone to talk with you about paying for help?

We adults don't want to need help nor do we want to admit we need it. Getting in touch with how it would be for you can help shape the conversation with your parent.

Your parent may have argued any of the following things when you brought up the subject of paid help:

1. I don't need help (not true)

2. I can't afford help (may not be true)

3. I don't want a stranger in my house (who would?)

Argument 1 – I Don't Need Help!

Think about this. Does Mom have a point? After all, if you're helping, that may be sufficient. Does she have a reason to ask you NOT to do so much?

If you keep taking her to appointments, doing her laundry, refilling her medications, she will let you. Rarely have I heard a parent say, "Hey, Honey, you don't need to do this. I'd like to start paying for help."

But really, this can be a tender subject. It may be painful for your parent to admit they need help, or they may have brain changes and don't recognize they need help. If you do the work, it can seem casual, as if you just love stopping by and doing things, and you may. For me, I got overwhelmed and missed my life.

Help with day to day activities can seem like a much more serious affair if your parent has to pay a stranger. I'm all for doing what you can to help. However, when it goes on for years, or morphs into helping a person shower, use the toilet, and so forth, it may be uncomfortable or even impossible.

Having paid home care employees is usually better than family help in the long run, because it allows you to keep or resume your normal role as son, daughter, spouse, or friend.

Here's a comparison your folks may understand. Most likely, they have paid for the professional services of a doctor, lawyer, dentist, or accountant over the years and not depended on you for these services. Couch the home help as another professional service.

If they remain resistant, stress that the help is for a specific chore or set amount of time. For example: Mom, I know you prefer that I help you, but this month I can't, sorry. We are going to use a home care professional for one month because:

- I need a break

- I'm scheduled for surgery

- I'm running away to join the circus

- Work is busy

- I want to be home when the kids get out of school

Argument 2 – I Can't Afford Help!

Money. The big pushback. Sometimes it's true that funds are limited and paid home care will be unrealistic. More often, though, there are funds, but a parent won't use them. Period. Consider, too, that your parent's changes may have been gradual, and they may think they are coping well. However, if they are declining, the question becomes: Can they afford the consequences of not having help?

Some consequences can be life threatening:

- Infections from being unclean due to lack of regular hygiene

- Food poisoning after eating bad food

- Medication errors, diabetic episodes

- Poor nutrition from not cooking or lacking fresh food

Other less risky consequences may be a smelly house because the garbage is not taken out, a filthy bathroom, dirty dishes in the sink, or maybe an overfed pet.

If finances are limited or a person has the assets but refuses to use them on home care, you have a couple of options.

You can pay for the home care yourself, as a gift. Or you can pay for the help now, knowing you may receive assets from the estate after your parent passes, which can be considered reimbursement.

If no one in the family can afford private home care, states may have a program to help. Go to Eldercare.ACL.Gov to get connected to what's available in your state.

Another solution to the argument of not wanting to pay for outside help can be that YOU get paid to help. It's not unreasonable to be paid for your continued help, especially if you have been sacrificing your day job. Your services have value!

Stop and ask yourself, how much do I want to do or continue to do? Would I feel better if I were paid to do this and if so, what compensation feels right? Tell your parent you will continue to help but your time is worth $_____ dollars per hour. Ask, "Would you be comfortable paying me that rate?"

DAD NOTES: I had a home care agency meet with my dad. During the visit, he learned that what I had been doing for nothing would cost $28.50 per hour. He signed on but never called them. When I pushed him to use the company, after scrubbing his bathroom on my hands and knees, he said, "I'll pay you forty dollars an hour," and he did. He passed away before we could call the home care company after that.

Argument 3 – I Don't Want A Stranger In My House!

Who does? But anyone is a stranger on the first visit. Even Mom's husband was a stranger when they met.

To soothe this concern, I recommend that you or another trusted person be present the first time the person from the home care organization comes to the home. You can help explain what is needed and help orient the caregiver. Most likely your parent will feel comfortable after that.

I have seen so many times where a parent balked at the idea of a helper initially and made family feel terrible and guilty. However, in time, the parent began to depend on the caregiver and looked forward to when they came and got upset if the caregiver didn't show. Give the relationship time to build.

Regardless of what topic you need to address with Mom or Dad, approach it in a loving way, but set your mind on a successful outcome. Don't be sheepish or casual when presenting the idea of paid care. If your parent senses you are not serious, they will rebuff the idea. If you have to, tell them you will reduce how often you visit until they get paid help.

E-mails with my friends:

Hi gals,
Got dad picked up from hospital today, on new heart medication but should be okay, I guess. I will be calling a home care agency to visit him and get registered so I can have backup. Whether he likes it or not! I was beyond the beyond this week with 5 days of caring.   Kira

Their responses:

Thanks for the update, Kir. I am so glad Dad is home for now. It is such an intense roller coaster time, and exhausting to the max as you being the point and only person. Woowee.
Rebecca

Glad you are setting things up to support Dad and yourself. That's what you taught me to do :) Love to both of you.
Cheryl

Chapter 18

Using Paid Help

You have two options when you can't or don't want to assist your parent: Hire someone privately OR hire an employee through a home care organization.

NOTE: This is not the same as a home health care company. That extra word "health" means that medical services are provided and Medicare covers them. That is doctor ordered. What you want is day-to-day non-medical assistance.

Option 1 – Private Hires

Hiring someone privately as your household employee can be done, but I don't recommend it. Hiring on your own adds many responsibilities such as interviewing candidates, running background checks, handling payroll, getting workers' compensation insurance, handling performance issues, filling in when the person doesn't show, and training when new needs surface.

If the person can't make the shift, moves, or quits, you will need to start over. That's a lot and can be exhausting. And remember, you're looking to lighten your load.

PITFALLS OF A PRIVATE HIRE: One adult daughter whose father had dementia told me about Lisa, a private caregiver who was doing a good job but had back pain and stopped coming. "I will never rely so heavily on one person again. My dad got used to Lisa coming, and while she was out, he went backward and declined. Even though we got someone to fill in, we were too long without help in between. When Lisa returned to work, Dad didn't interact with her in the same way. He refused to go out of the house with her anymore."

Option 2 – Use a Home Care Organization

There are many home care organizations to choose from that provide nonmedical help. To find a company, look online under "Home Care" or ask friends for a recommendation.

You can choose companionship and personal care services such as:

- Help with bathing and dressing
- Prepare grocery lists and shop
- Plan, prepare, and clean up meals
- Help arrange appointments
- Assist with walking and getting in and out of bed
- Reminisce
- Alzheimer's care
- Medication reminders
- Transportation
- Light housekeeping
- Help to toilet
- Pick up prescriptions
- Laundry
- Make bed and change linens
- Play games, discuss current events, play music

Screening Companies

Call a couple of companies to see how responsive they are in the first exchange. Go with the one that seems best to you. Ask if they are licensed. If so, you know they are meeting the state requirements.

Once you provide information about your parent to the organization, they will schedule a time to meet and review services they offer and pricing. They will learn of any particular needs and then ask your parent to sign the service contract.

It's that easy. Your parent can now begin with a caregiver. The organization sends someone whom they think matches what your parent needs. However, if your parent prefers, ask if they can send potential caregivers to meet, so your parent may choose. Some organizations I have worked with charge for this interview time and some don't.

First Days Using a Home Care Organization

Have the employee make the initial visit with the intent of building rapport with your parent. Once your parent seems comfortable, they can begin doing tasks.

NOTE: If your parent has some memory loss or confusion, you might want to be present during the first few shifts the caregiver works. To decrease the threat of someone in the home, it's okay to tell your parent that the person is a friend of yours. If the two get along, then on the next visit your "friend" can be there without you.

Begin with chores that don't involve personal care, if feasible. Simple tasks like washing dishes, taking out the garbage, or preparing a snack are good places to start. Consider your parent's perspective and pace. It's unlikely you would want to run an errand with a stranger you just met or have them help dress you. Do what is comfortable.

Be sure to have more than one employee work shifts, if possible. This way there is an alternate helper your parent will know. The primary caregiver your parent likes and depends on may get sick, need a vacation, or leave. The industry has a lot of turnover, unfortunately. But the good news is that the company can easily send others when this happens.

The home care organization typically provides a binder with instructions for the staff and forms for employees to document what they do on their shifts. Feel free to review this binder, and what the employees write, so you have a sense of how things are going. This is not just for employees. You can add a note, so caregivers coming on shift can read it.

Consider creating a "do and don't list" so all caregivers coming into the house know the rules. If your parent wants to make the bed, write, "Please don't make bed, Dad will do this task."

Be prepared for your parent to fire the caregiver and for you to feel defeated or angry. It may take several tries to find the right person(s) to care for your parent. Don't give up just because one experience didn't work. You get better at interviewing and knowing what will work. Stick with it and don't let your parent push away other caregivers without giving them a try. Parents are sometimes looking for a reason to make the situation not work because they want you. It's normal. Hold your ground.

It's important to keep in regular touch with the home care organization to discuss changes over time. You're acting as supervisor, in a way.

If for any reason the caregivers are not performing as you think they should, feel free to discuss concerns with the home care supervisor or ask for a different employee. Communication is your friend. Don't suffer through! You are paying for this service and it should meet your needs. If the company is unable to find reliable, competent staff, call another one.

I like to provide a personal history fact sheet about the person for employees. It helps the caregivers learn a little bit about whom they are caring for, so that they will be able to engage with your parent in specific, meaningful ways.

On the next page is a wonderful example of what one client family created for caregivers to read about their mom. If you read this, wouldn't you know how to interact in a more meaningful way?

Thanks to Mrs. Louvar's family for graciously allowing me to share so others may benefit.

Theresa Louvar - November 26, 1921

Born in Brooklyn, NY

Attended beauty school after high school

Married 40 years to _____ deceased 1982

Married 11 years to_____ deceased 1999

3 children _____ and daughter in law_____

5 grandchildren

4 great-grandchildren

Very proud about being a businesswoman

Don't talk about money with her, makes her anxious

Concerned about the cost of living at assisted living home

Reply with, "It costs the same as where you just moved from."

Loves to paint on canvas, do ceramics

Loves the Travel Channel

Has an elephant collection

Likes to go out to dine with her family

Escort to meals

Needs supervision on outings

Likes to hold hands

Has a friend named _____ from _____ who will visit her

Is very social and likes to hear people's life stories

Gets her hair done once a week

Gets a manicure every week

Gets a pedicure once a month

Uses Oil of Olay facial wipes to clean her face daily

Can become agitated and strike out

Usually sleeps well at night

Will need supervision going to bathroom at night to prevent falls

Chapter 19

Driving

Maybe you think your parent shouldn't be driving but they don't seem to notice or acknowledge the same dangers and concerns. They may think that because they have driven for 50+ years, they're fine. And some people age and drive well right to the end of their lives. Some of us impose restrictions on ourselves that make sense, such as not driving in the rain, or at night, or on the freeway.

But, if your parent is having fender benders or their car is scraped and they aren't sure how it happened, or you're afraid to drive with them, it's time to plan how to address safer driving.

Families can be hesitant to address the subject of driving, fearing they will be met with resistance, hostility, and denial. Driving represents freedom and having that threatened is difficult. It can be stressful to know how to approach the subject. The conversation is truly about the big loss of independence that can come from not driving, and it's rare that someone wants to stop driving.

This is another one of those times where you need to put yourself in their shoes. What would you do if I said YOU can't drive anymore? It's crucial to consider how that feels before talking with your parent about limiting or stopping driving.

Also, before you talk, have some ideas of transit alternatives. Are you going to take them places? Will another be driving them? Will a person be paid to drive? Will you call a taxi, Lyft, or Uber?

Will you learn public transportation routes together? It's easier for your parent to give up driving if they have alternatives.

If this conversation is too difficult for you to have, hire a geriatric care manager to have it for you.

Options for Addressing Driving Concerns

If you're worried your parent shouldn't be driving, it's good to know that there are a few options to address your concerns before just taking the keys away:

A. Your parent can take the Safe Driver course offered by AARP to update their skills and knowledge. The class helps to increase driving safety and confidence. After they complete the course, you can see if their driving improved.

I took the course myself and learned many things such as: daily exercise can improve driving-related movements, many factors negatively affect me when I'm tired and driving (more than I realized) and that I am supposed to allow three seconds between myself and the car in front of me instead of one car length per 10 miles per hour I learned decades ago. Also, by taking the course I lowered my car insurance cost.

AARP also offers a free online seminar called We Need to Talk that will help you determine how to assess your loved ones' driving skills and provide tools to help you have this important conversation. Go to AARP.org/weneedtotalk.

Check out their driving resource center AARP.org/DRC for more tools and classes.

B. See if your state offers a Car Fit program. This program provides assistive devices so drivers can feel more comfortable in the driver's seat. Car-Fit.org.

Your parent can be evaluated by an Occupational Therapist. That professional can assess how they operate the car and make suggestions that may address concerns. Look online or ask the doctor for an Occupational Therapist recommendation.

In northern California, a resource is the Driver Cognitive Assessment Center, DCACBAYAREA.com, (925) 249-5947.

C. Your parent can apply for a Restricted License. In this scenario, DMV comes to their home and your parent is responsible for giving them a map of places they routinely drive to.

IF your parent can demonstrate to DMV that they can safely manage the "area drive," they can have a Restricted License to do so. The parameters for when and where they can drive are actually put on the license, in case they are stopped by a police officer. A Restricted License may mean they can't go on the freeway, or drive at night, or drive to farther away places, but it's better than having no license at all.

D. Your loved one can be visited by a calm, trained professional for an in-home, enhanced self-assessment and conversation about their driving. The incredible outcome is that after the conversation and evaluation, the majority of people decide to give up the car keys!

Visit BeyondDrivingWithDignity.com to see if the program is offered in your state.

Get a State ID from DMV

If your parent's driver's license has expired, get a state ID. Having a valid state ID is needed to sign legal documents such as a trust or power of attorney.

Prepare for the Day Your Parent May Not be Able to Drive

Begin driving your parent places BEFORE they start to have driving problems, so they get used to your driving. This establishes a safe routine at a time when they can still drive and their ego or pride are less likely to be involved.

I worked this into the fabric of my relationship with my dad, so the habit became familiar. I'd call him and say, "Hey, I'm going to stop by and pick you up so we can grocery shop." Or, "I'm in your neighborhood and hungry, how about we grab lunch together? I'll stop by and pick you up." It became so routine for me to pick him up that he didn't even offer to pick me up anymore. I did this way before he was too weak to drive.

Dementia Dangers When Driving

If your parent already has dementia when you become aware that they should not be driving, you may have to come up with a different plan.

You have probably heard of cases in the news when a person with dementia ends up hundreds of miles from their home. This means they drove away and got so confused they could not get home so they kept driving. I can't imagine how frightened the drivers (and families) are when this happens.

Time to act on behalf of us all for public safety.

You may have to take away all the copies of the car keys.

Some families disconnect the starter from the car, so it appears broken to the parent with dementia, deterring them from driving. However, there are instances where a person with dementia has called a mechanic to come to the home to fix the car or has even gone out and purchased a new car!

You may try an excuse such as a relative's car broke down and they need to borrow your parent's for a while. That time can be extended until your parent gets used to someone else driving.

You can pretend something needs servicing on the car and remove it from the property. Sometimes not seeing the car reduces the thoughts of driving. If asked, you can explain over and over that the car is being serviced. Hopefully your parent forgets and eventually stops asking about the car.

Sometimes you can ask your parent if they want to give their car to a grandchild or relative as a present, so the parent feels good about not having a car rather than upset.

You may need to tell their doctor your concerns so that the doctor can evaluate your parent's cognitive status and notify DMV if there is dementia. The doctor is mandated to report a patient with dementia symptoms to them so the DMV can ask your parent into their office for further evaluation.

You may have to make an online report to DMV. Some states allow it to be an anonymous report.

What happens when DMV is notified?

They send a notice saying they have been made aware the person has a condition which may affect driving and the license is now suspended. The letter asks the person to come into DMV to be evaluated.

At DMV, the person has to answer questions in writing and orally to prove their driving knowledge.

If they pass that part, they are asked to do a driving test.

If they pass, and they just might, the license is reinstated.

If they do not pass, the license remains suspended and later revoked.

Be prepared that your parent may insist on driving anyway, license or no license. You may need to move the car off the property, hide the keys, or notify the police that your parent is driving on a suspended license. I wish there could just be a boot put on the car so the stress was not on families to manage this issue, but the DMV doesn't do that. . . yet.

This can be a difficult time so remember that a care manager can work with your parent to figure out new methods for transportation instead of you, if you wish.

Chapter 20

Dementia Tips

This chapter is meant to provide key nuggets to help if your loved one has some form of dementia.

It's said that caring for someone with dementia is more difficult than caring for someone with a physical problem. Care can certainly take more time.

Knowing someone one way for years and years, and then having their brain change, which leads to a change in behavior and memory, can be very painful to witness. To help you remain patient I recommend you learn to understand these changes.

Caregivers can get resentful while caregiving and if a relationship has been challenging to begin with, having a loved one with dementia can exacerbate the anger. Some people find a way to figure out this journey, and some want to divorce themselves from the situation.

As exhausted or frustrated as you may be feeling, you have to learn about this new place – Planet Dementia – and how things operate there. Don't wing it. The sooner you learn how to handle behaviors, understand how your loved one is now perceiving the world with a broken brain, and what their strengths are and how to capitalize on them, the better. It's vital to gain knowledge about the way dementia changes the brain.

I like to remind families that just because a person has dementia that does not mean the person is now dumb. Being dumb is not the same as not remembering or needing assistance to handle day-to-day affairs.

Having a professional eldercare manager will help you a great deal. We can provide the education and resources to get you through, see Chapter 2. There are webinars, books, classes, support groups, and you can call the Alzheimer's Association Helpline 24 hours a day (800) 272-3900, Alz.org.

You will need to hear the tips and tricks over and over to begin to integrate them, because YOU need to behave in a new way.

10 Warning Signs by the Alzheimer's Association

It's important to note that we now recognize that one of the first signs of dementia is having difficulty managing financial affairs.

That can mean not opening bills that come in the mail, or not even recognizing what bills are. It can mean not paying bills on time or paying them twice. This can lead to a financial mess for you to clean up.

1. Memory loss that disrupts daily life

2. Challenges in planning or solving problems

3. Difficulty completing familiar tasks

4. Confusion with time or place

5. Trouble understanding visual images and spatial relationships

6. New problems with words in speaking or writing

7. Misplacing things and losing the ability to retrace steps

8. Decreased or poor judgment

9. Withdrawal from work or social activities

10. Changes in mood and personality

Emotions Are Critical

I believe a person with dementia continues to recognize emotions expressed by others, as though their spidey sense remains (and research shows that our emotional brain remains intact, meaning emotion gets through to us). So, if you or another person is mean towards them, they may not recall what happened, but they will remember feeling bad or afraid. Do your best to have interactions with smiles and love. I know this is not easy to do, but to maintain the integrity and trust with your loved one, it's a key thing to strive toward. David Troxel wrote *The Best Friend's Approach to Alzheimer's Care,* and he promotes treating your loved one like a friend. If you wouldn't speak to your friend in a harsh way, that can help you remember to be kind with your loved one.

Compassionate Communication

I see many families argue with parents who have dementia. They think they can talk sense into a person who has memory loss and confusion. Usually we try explaining things to someone with logic in order to accomplish tasks and communication, but people with dementia can experience changes in vision, hearing, and processing data that makes logic unsuccessful. To make matters more confusing, sometimes your parent is having a good spell and seems to take everything in and agree with all you're saying, only to change their mind or deny they agreed with you earlier. This is not deliberate. They are doing the best they can.

As a caregiver, it's hard to feel successful as your parent has worsening symptoms. But, imagine how your parent feels, especially if they can't express their sadness, needs or frustration with words.

People with dementia need to feel safe and protected at all times, so let that guide you when working with them.

What to Do When Your Loved One has Dementia

- Be brave and tell the doctor, or others, how difficult the behaviors are at home.

- Try medications; consider medical cannabis for behavior management.

- Try having your loved one attend a day club program.

- Arrange for your loved one to move to an assisted living community offering memory care, if only for a respite stay of 30 to 60 days, so you can get a break.

- Ask friends or members of an organization or house of worship your parent once attended if they could come and reminisce or take a walk with your loved one. One tennis club had volunteers walk each day with a former club member who now had dementia.

Dementia experts will often encourage you to take care of yourself so you can go the distance caring for someone else, and this is key. To take care of yourself, you may need to arrange time alone. You may need to have others stay with your loved one so you can be away from them. It's healthy to have these breaks, so please don't feel guilty. And yes, your loved one may be more comfortable with you around, but they will adjust to someone else, especially if it's on a consistent schedule.

Moving a Person with Dementia

I suggest a person aging alone with dementia be moved to a supportive living environment such as an assisted living community offering memory care if one of the following factors is at play:

- They are isolated

- They are lonely

- They are unsafe

- They are unable to pay for enough help to remain at home

When a person can't live alone anymore, usually they have progressed from mild to moderate dementia. They may no longer shower or take medication correctly. They may be unable to heat a meal or make appointments. They may even leave their home for a walk and not know how to return.

Working with a placement agency or care manager to arrange a move can be very helpful. They have handled moves multiple times and know how to manage the worries before, during, and after a move. A care manager can be the person who transports your loved one to the care home, so you don't have to be there that day.

It's a good idea to let your parent take the lead with asking questions. If they are not asking questions, it's okay not to provide much information about a move. They may not be able to process what you tell them, so don't feel obligated to review all the details. It will be your demeanor that informs them, so try to be calm and matter of fact about changes.

Please refrain from threatening your loved one with a move. It doesn't work to say, "If you keep doing this behavior, you won't be able to stay here, you'll have to go to a nursing home!" A person with dementia can't control their behavior, so this rationale doesn't work. You will feel worse in the end if you try this, so stop sentences like that before they leave your lips.

Going Home

Many of my clients with dementia who have moved, tell family they want to go home, over and over. This can be heartbreaking to hear and to know how to respond. However, I have observed that home appears to be just a place in their mind where the world made sense, not an actual location. I had one family actually move their mom back to her childhood home in Ohio (from California) only to have her say "I want to go home" when she was there, too.

Phone Calls

If you are getting frequent calls all day long, your parent is probably using you as a reassuring connection throughout the day. This may be hard on you.

There are a couple of remedies. You can get a cell phone that is dedicated to your parent's calls only. You give your parent THAT phone number and then you know all calls coming to that number are from your parent and no one else. You can leave a soothing out-going message that your parent hears over and over when they call. When you are able to return their call, you do.

You may want to get call forwarding for your parent's home phone and forward those calls to your number. This way no spam, scam, or important phone calls will be answered by your parent. You will get those calls and be able to manage them.

For incoming calls you do want your parent to answer from friends, relatives, spiritual helpers, etc., consider getting a cell phone for your parent and letting their network have that number to reach your parent.

Outings

Many people with dementia begin to refuse to leave their house, even to places they have always gone and enjoyed. They may make a lot of excuses for not going out that you want to challenge. I believe the outside world can get a bit too big and is harder to make sense of when you have dementia. It can be hard for someone with dementia to imagine where they are going, what will be inside a store or restaurant, or even the reason for going. A trip to the store can be met with "I don't need anything there." If this happens, don't insist they join you. People are taking care of themselves without knowing how to tell you. Honor that.

Also, when your parent needs to go out, you don't need to give much advance notice. In fact, too much notice can cause worry. The person can experience anxiety if they're anticipating the outing, the time, or the purpose. Just say," I'll be picking you up in an hour, can you be dressed by then?" Learning to give fewer explanations can be hard since we normally communicate with more details. But since the brain of the person with dementia may not be able to handle many details, it's okay to leave them out.

There can be a lot of tears and emotion when your parent is no longer acting like a parent and won't return to who they always were to you. Feel free to shed those tears and disappointment while getting the support you need to carry on. Check out the list of other dementia resources in the RESOURCES section of this book.

Final Thoughts

Thank you for reading my book. I hope it provides helpful advice that makes caregiving more manageable. Please take care of yourself in the process. I hope, too, that you recognize and appreciate the smiles, the hugs, and the love that you help nurture. In my eyes you are a quiet hero.

Closing notes on Dad: I asked my dad, who lived alone, to move closer to me as he aged. I'm grateful he agreed. I suggest this to clients all the time because being nearby makes caregiving so much easier.

He said he loved the place he moved to in my small town, and I was glad I didn't need to drive to San Francisco to see him and care for him at a distance.

Before the last two intense months of his cancer treatments, there were lots of Chinese lunches we shared and yummy dinners, Willits trips, poker games, times on the beach, and hugs and kisses. He was my go-to pal a lot of times.

I thought he was doing me a favor by moving close by, but he helped me too. Our caring was mutual. Having my dad a few minutes away as an adult brought a new dimension to our relationship. The connection we developed from that ease of seeing each other is a treasured time and I got more than I ever thought possible during the last six years of his life.

I hope your experience transforms your relationship for the better, even if it takes time to see that it did.

Resources

Books

A Dignified Life: The Best Friends Approach to Alzheimer's Care;
Virginia Bell, MSW and David Troxel, MPH.
Best Friends™ Health Professions Press, 2020

Coping with Behavior Change in Dementia;
Spencer and White. Dementiacarebooks.com

Moving a Relative and Other Transitions in Dementia Care;
Spencer and White. Dementiacarebooks.com, 2019

*The Patient's Checklist: 10 Simple Hospital Checklists to Keep You Safe,
Sane and Organized;* Elizabeth Bailey. Sterling Publishing, 2011

Mom Loves You Best: Forgiving and Forging Sibling Relationships;
Cathy Cress and Kali Cress Peterson. New Horizon Press, 2010

How to Care for Aging Parents;
Virginia Morris. Workman Publishing, 2014

Estate Planning for the Sandwich Generation;
Catherine Hodder, Esq. 2018

Essential Retirement Planning for Solo Agers;
Sara Zeff Geber, PhD. 2018

The Family Guide to Aging Parents;
Carolyn Rosenblatt. 2015

Stages of Senior Care: Your Step-by-Step Guide to Making the Best Decisions; Paul and Lori Hogan. McGraw-Hill, 2010

Stop Caretaking the Borderline or Narcissist: How to End the Drama and Get On with Life; Margalis Fjelstad. Rowman & Littlefield Publishers, Inc., 2013

Loving Hard-to-Love Parents: A Handbook for Adult Children of Difficult Older Parents; Paul K. Chafetz, PhD, 2017. PaulKChafetz.com

No Regrets: Hope for Your Caregiving Season; Rayna Neises. Morgan James Publishing, 2021

Travel Well With Dementia by Jan Doughterty

The Busy Caregiver's Guide to Advanced Alzheimer's Disease by Jennifer R. Stelter, PsyD

Movies

The Savages – Siblings have to care for a father they never liked. A serious comedy.

Two Weeks – Mom is terminal; adult children come to be with her. Humorous and relatable.

Still Alice – Story of a renowned linguistics professor and mom of three grown children who develops early-onset Alzheimer's disease.

Trouble with the Curve – If the classic Clint Eastwood is like your dad, then this movie is for you. He's salty and not happy about the fact that aging may be starting to affect him.

Websites

Kira's website, CallKira.com

Kira's YouTube channel of videos
https://www.youtube.com/channel/UCyO7atbCToRbKmnFI6EZGAg

Veterans Care Coordination: Help obtaining the pension
with Aid and Attendance benefit
https://vcchc.com/

Aging Life Care Association: to locate an aging life care manager in the U.S.
https://www.aginglifecare.org//

TechEnhancedLife.com article: Care Managers: What, Why, For Whom?

TechEnhancedLife.com, evaluations written by older adults about
products and services, designed for older adults, that they have tested

National Academy of Elder Law Attorneys, NAELA.org

Alz.org, resources and education about dementias

Bestfriendsapproach.com, techniques to care for someone with dementia

TeepaSnow.com, dementia expert provides tools and resources for caring

Information on Adverse Drug Reactions
from The Centers for Disease Control and Prevention
cdc.gov/MedicationSafety/

Family Caregiving and Out-of-Pocket Costs
https://www.aarp.org/caregiving/financial-legal/info-2019/
out-of-pocket-costs.html?intcmp=AE-CRC-TOENG-TOGL

CFAD.org, Caring from a Distance

CaringToday.com, support for caregivers

Sandwich Generation Issues
https://www.seniorliving.org/caregiving/sandwich-generation/

About the Author

Kira Reginato is a CMC (Care Manager Certified) and eldercare consultant. Kira has served thousands of older adults and their families in a variety of settings, including hospitals, residential care facilities, skilled nursing facilities, hospices, an Alzheimer's adult day care program, and Meals on Wheels. In 2007, she opened the eldercare management firm, **Living Ideas for Elders.**

By the time Kira was in high school, she knew she wanted to work with older adults. She attributes this to her close relationship with her paternal grandma.

For five years, Kira hosted a live weekly radio show called **The Elder Care Show,** which was later renamed **Call Kira About Aging.** The show featured interviews with guests who were specialists in the field of aging and caregiving. Topics included veteran's benefits, sex over 60, dementia, assisted living, and many others. Podcasts of the shows are available at **CallKira.com.**

Kira also helped develop an app for family caregivers called the **Caring App.** The app answers 170 commonly asked eldercare questions and provides a platform for keeping track of multiple aspects of an older adult's life.

Contact Kira Reginato

P.O. Box 543, Sebastopol, CA 95473-0543

Phone: (707) 762-5433

Email: Kira@callkira.com

Website: CallKira.com

LinkedIn: CallKiraAboutAging

CallKira.com

To order a copy of this book
for a relative or friend,
visit CallKira.com
or Amazon.com.

Amazon.com

Get the package of the checklists and questionnaires
in this book in 8 1/2" x 11" format to make them easier
to complete and to include copies in your binders.

Made in USA - Kendallville, IN
46361_9798748826273
02.09.2023 1320